Transforming
Schools

A Social Perspective

Transforming Schools

A Social Perspective

Charlotte P. Taylor

ST. MARTIN'S PRESS   NEW YORK

Library of Congress Catalog Card Number: 75-38022
Copyright © 1976 by St. Martin's Press, Inc.
All Rights Reserved.
Manufactured in the United States of America.
09876
fedcba
For information, write: St. Martin's Press, Inc.,
175 Fifth Avenue, New York, N. Y. 10010

Preface

The traditional task of schools has been to transform children into the sorts of adults their society desires. As the twentieth century opened, progressive educators challenged schools to change society as well. Now, as the twentieth century draws to a close, schools themselves must be transformed in order to prepare youth for a variety of possible future societies.

The traditional method of the schools, transmitting knowledge of and from the past, is decreasingly fruitful because the society that created the American school system is going through rapid change not matched in the school system itself. In short, there is a lag between what our society's members need to know and what the schools choose to teach. This situation has arisen either because the majority of American educators are ignorant of the interdependence of education and society, or because they believe they should shield the day-by-day activities of pupils from the realities of twentieth-century life.

To provide a foundation in sociological fact and theory is one way to sensitize new educators to the reality of society in and from which schools derive their purpose and function. I prepared this volume to help my students understand the nature of this interactive system of school and society and thus become better able to transform the schools in which they will teach. So *Transforming Schools: A Social Perspective* is dedicated to them, and to other future teachers, parents, and citizens who care about education.

A major inspiration for my structuralist view of American education has been the British text *An Introduction to the Sociology of Education*, by Brian J. Ashley, Harry S. Cohen, and Roy G. Slatter. Their utilization of Talcott Parsons' model of social interaction led to the development of this "second generation" structuralist interpretation, and I acknowledge my deep indebtedness to them.

Thanks are also due to Lucille Smith and Margaret Eldredge for typing and retyping the manuscript; to Verlie Gaither and Stanley Gale for verifying sources; to my friends for their interest and my family for their loving support.

CHARLOTTE P. TAYLOR

Contents

Transforming
Schools
A Social Perspective

Introduction

Where does the money come from to pay your salary as a
   teacher?
Who determines what you will teach?
Do boys want to achieve in schools as much as do girls?
Is it legal to prohibit student publications?

If you were to ask the future teachers sitting beside you in an
educational foundations class these questions, you would probably get some wrong answers or some incomplete answers but
very few knowledgeable answers. How well could you answer
them?

The American public-school system is pushed and shoved and
is constantly interacting with the political, economic, and social
institutions surrounding it. Decisions made by governments,
labor unions, churches, and other institutions influence *who* is
taught *what*. On their part, schools are expected to provide
reciprocal support for the other parts of society. For example,
they are expected to prepare active citizens and trainable
workers. These ongoing, transforming interactions continuously
affect schools but are almost never studied in the schools
themselves. Most students, administrators, and teachers proceed as if the schools existed in an isolation chamber, free of the

germs of "real life." This paradox may be one reason why many recent public-school graduates condemn their education as "irrelevant." As students, they seldom saw a connection between what went on in school and what they would need to know as members of society.

As we come to the end of the twentieth century, American society and all its social institutions are undergoing very rapid change. Today few schools are responding to these changes; tomorrow they must respond or die. If schools are to cope with the challenges of the future, we must transform schools by improving their sensitivity and effectiveness in dealing with social reality. Teachers need to see the school as enmeshed in a web of transactions with other institutions of society. This will permit teachers to better understand the *why* and *how* of their own institution of society, education, and, more particularly, the schools. The purpose of this text is to help you gain this view by studying the sociological foundations of education.

Unfortunately, some college professors continue the isolation of the schools. This has been so true traditionally that we have a term to describe it—the "ivory tower." Scholars may be busy there, but they infrequently look out at the troops besieging the gates. You and your teachers are going to have to work hard to break through the walls that surround your schooling so that you may be realistically educated. Books and theory bring perspective, but your own future pupils are flesh and blood. To bring alive the issues you will be facing as a teacher, you will need exposure to current and firsthand social realities by way of field trips; practicums; analyses of TV, movies, and daily newspapers; special speakers from the state legislature, the courts, and "the streets." Experiences like these can provide a laboratory to practice the skills of analysis and application that you will need in your profession. Suggestions for activities like these are found at the end of each chapter. By no means should you limit yourself to these.

Obviously then, this little volume is not intended to be your sole resource in studying the sociological foundations of education. In order to make sense of the practical experiences you will have, however, you will need to relate them one to another in some meaningful way. Other scholars before you have developed a variety of frameworks to use in understanding experiences in society. History, economics, and psychology represent three disciplines whose individual theories might be used to explain a single act of human behavior. The discipline of sociology provides its own structure for understanding transactions involving persons, groups, and social institutions.

In the following pages, sociological concepts provide a model that is like a blueprint of a house. Using this model, you can sort facts you learn until you have a logical structure in your own mind that resembles the larger structure of society. The words that introduce particularly important concepts are italicized in the text and can be found in a glossary at the end of the chapter in which they first appear. Further, in order to encourage your active mental involvement, the text is occasionally interrupted by questions asking you to give examples from your own experience or to relate one piece of information to another.

That last sentence expresses a key concept of this book. You can perhaps "teach" in the ivory tower; but in real life, you cannot be "learned." The initiation for learning must be in your hands. After twelve or more years in the American public-school system, this may be a very difficult concept for you to grasp. You will find this idea presented many times on the following pages. It is the cornerstone of transforming schools.

In this book you will also find theoretical concepts and some historical background. Examples of unique school procedures will put some flesh on the framework. To this you must add many practical experiences like those mentioned above. You should make a special effort to begin to establish the habit of being alert and responsive to the news of the day. That's where it's happening—tomorrow hurrying toward today.

This book uses one particular model to analyze and synthesize facts and concepts about education. It is not the only way of interpreting social interaction. So, rather than absorbing it wholesale, use it as a tool to construct your own mental model of social reality. When your model is finished, you will be well on your way to becoming a more effective teacher with a better preparation for changing the schools in which you work.

Society, Structure, and System

THE NATURE OF GROUPS AND SCHOOL GROUPS

People establish groups in order to accomplish a purpose that they cannot accomplish as individuals acting alone. A married couple wishes to establish a legal and lasting home for children they may have. Two hundred million persons wish to govern themselves in a group called the United States of America. Every group exists to get something done that could not be done by individual members on their own. A group may have more than one purpose. But groups die away if members feel the group has no purpose to hold them together.

The field of sociology deals with the general behavior of human beings in groups. When sociologists focus upon an individual, they are most interested in that person's role in the groups to which he or she belongs. Social institutions such as government and economics interest sociologists because they are huge webs of persons and groups interacting in a variety of roles.

The sociology of education focuses particularly on those groups called schools. What is the purpose of schools? Specifically, it is to help *socialize* members of society; that is, they help bring about changes in the behavior of new, and usually young, members of society (the group that supports the school) so that they will be acceptable members of that society. Different schools emphasize different outcomes, but all engage in the shared activity of *socialization*, as the process is called. Public schools want educated citizens; parochial schools, religious devotees; dancing schools, better dancers. To become fully human, children must learn how to behave in society. The family has the first and primary responsibility for socialization; the schools are expected to complement and continue the process. All the many goals and activities of a school can be related to this basic purpose: socialization.

Of course, much planned and incidental education goes on in any society outside of its schools. For instance, where did you learn about the "Top Forty" tunes, the Old West, your religious heritage, and Grandma's recipe for apple pie? Some of these other educative forces must be considered, especially when they modify what happens in schools. When the mass media, such as television and the movies, or religious organizations focus primarily on socialization, they are part of the social institution of education. *Peer groups*—those people whom you consider your equals and whose habits you tend to adopt as your own—are also a major socializing institution. But schools, especially publicly established schools, are center-stage in American education and also in the concerns of this book.

There are three different levels of groups to consider when we talk about schools: groups of students called classes, groups of classes called schools, and the system of schools that as a part of the institution of education fits into the larger system of society as a whole. In this book all three levels of school groups and how each level affects the others will be examined.

THE ACTIVITIES OF GROUPS

Sociologists have noted that no matter what the size or task of a group, in order to get its main purpose accomplished, each group must do certain things. It is possible, therefore, to assume about group activities that "general laws concerning group life can be discovered which will hold for such apparently different groups as a juvenile gang, . . . a jury and a railroad maintenance crew." (Dorwin Cartwright and Alvin Zander, 1960, p. 38)

There are four functions every group must accomplish in order to perform its purpose:

1. Decision making: defining the goals (ends and means) of the group
2. Allocation: assigning members to roles within the group
3. Integration: delivering sanctions to protect the group's survival
4. Socialization: establishing norms of behavior for individual members

Naturally, these common group activities have received much attention from sociologists and as we define and describe them, we will introduce concepts used throughout this discipline.

Decision Making: Defining the Goals of the Group

There is a task to be accomplished. The group is together because members realize that—but how can they get it done? What steps ought to be taken? What solution is better than another? How do we get from here to there? How can we improve the elementary reading program? What materials are available? Should we use one or many methods? How will we retrain the teachers? You can see the group has to make many subdecisions about means and intermediate ends in order to accomplish its overall purpose.

The definition of the goals of the group is frequently determined by the nature of its leadership—who makes decisions and how. Leadership in animal groups may be by sheer brute force. Human groups seldom select their leaders that way. Even in juvenile gangs, personal success in fighting is less important than being wise in the ways of the street. As human history has progressed, fewer decisions are made by the chief or wise man acting alone. Human decisions are frequently made by many group members, each taking a part in deciding various aspects of the decision. A single leader usually does not have all the knowledge needed for the complicated choices modern humans must make.

Allocation: *Assigning Members to Roles*

Once the goals have been defined, the means of accomplishing them are divided up among the members. This process involves allocating or placing people in certain positions, or roles, in order to get a job done. Sociologists define *roles* as expectations of behavior that the group sets up to get a particular job done regardless of what person does the job. That is, the group determines what ought to be done in that position. Among penguins, this means that the male sits on the egg while the female forages for food. Animals are frequently given *assigned roles* by group members on the basis of age, or sex, or size. Humans also use these criteria. To play the role of a citizen, you must attain a certain age. However, most human roles demand ability to perform much more specific behavior than the simple tasks of animals. You are enrolled in this course to learn more specific behavior for your future role as a teacher.

You may not yet have met your mathematics professor—but you certainly do not expect her to walk into the classroom, prop her feet on the radiator, and take a nap until the bell rings for the next class. Your expectation of her behavior is already structured and defined just because she fills the role of a college teacher. And because of your expectation, however much she may wish to nap, her behavior is probably controlled by the role assigned to her.

A characteristic of roles is that they are frequently reciprocal; that is, the role one person is given often complements the roles of others in the group. Thus what a professor does often structures what you as a student will do (see Figure 1.1). Of course, this will also be true when you are a teacher. Can you identify now what expectations you hold for your students, as yet unknown to you except that each will be fulfilling the role of "student"? What does your expectation of their behavior in the student role imply about your behavior in the teaching role?

Figure 1.1 Variations in the Flow of Communication Behavior Due to Variations in Student-Professor Reciprocal Roles

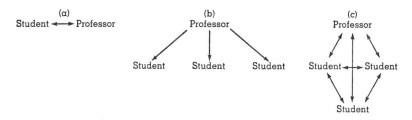

Example (a) might represent the tutorial system, where a single teacher and a single student mutually discuss a student project.

Example (b) might represent a typical lecture. The professor does all the talking; the students' reciprocal behavior is to remain silent and not communicate verbally.

Example (c) might represent a discussion group in which the students speak not only to the professor (and he with them) but also to each other.

Roles are not only reciprocal on a one-to-one basis; they also fit into other complex webs of human interaction. There are, for example, over 20,000 different kinds of jobs in the American economic system. The role of the production factory worker is linked to that of the salesperson or clerk, to the housewife who consumes the product, and the banker who invests the profit. A major expectation of American schools is that they will prepare workers for these various occupational roles. Society believes that by different kinds of academic preparation, schools ought to assign students to roles in our economic system. This assignment to an occupational role is called the *allocating function* of schools. It represents a major reason for the support of public schools in our country.

Roles do not describe only working behaviors. Were you surprised when the pronoun "she" was used for a college professor? Your expectations of the sex roles may have been jolted. Much of the tension of the women's liberation movement has come from a revision in the behaviors we expect of a female in her many roles as woman, employee, wife, and mother. Schools are sometimes expected to train for these sorts of behavioral expectations as well as for vocational roles.

Because one person may fulfill a variety of roles, there is sometimes conflict in his or her attempts to meet a variety of role expectations. In Chapter 6, much school behavior will be analyzed as resulting from conflict in role behaviors.

Integration: Delivering Sanctions to Protect the Group's Survival

The activities of defining goals and assigning roles deal directly with getting the group's task accomplished. But in order to get the job done, the group must stay together. Individual members cannot drop out in order to pursue an activity that is more immediately rewarding to them individually. For example, compulsory attendance laws aim to guarantee that students will be physically present as part of the school group. Maintaining the life of the group itself as a unit, at least until the purpose that brought it together is accomplished, is as vital a function of the group as the accomplishment of the task itself. If the group dis-integrates, its purpose will never be accomplished.

Traditionally, keeping members within the group has been accomplished by punishing or threatening to punish any member whose behavior threatens the health or survival of the group. Because of this, the notion of *sanctions* has come to have a fairly negative connotation. The concept, however, also includes positive supports for membership behavior as well. When we speak of delivering sanctions to integrate the group, we mean exerting group pressures to hold members together.

In many societies, laws to perpetuate that society are established that may last over the lifetimes of many individual members. These laws proscribe (prohibit) some behaviors and prescribe (require) some others. Elaborate judicial systems are set up to deliver and carry out negative sanctions against those who do not behave as the group has decided its survival requires. This is true whether it is the Supreme Court of the United States determining the constitutionality of a lower court decision, or Little League officials demanding that players wear matching uniforms.

Positive sanctions in the form of rewards are also used to

encourage desired behavior. Presumably, the key to the executive restroom makes a new manager more loyal to his or her company.

Socialization: Establishing Norms of Behavior

Sanctions are group processes to bring about desired behavior. Human animals, however, with their intense self-consciousness, make far superior group members if they *desire* to act as members of the group and follow intrinsically the behavior society approves. Time and attention given to sanctioning is time and energy that cannot be spent in the group's task. If members willingly acquiesce to the expectations of society, the group purpose is accomplished more efficiently and with less internal strain. The process of defining and inculcating in individual members socially preferred behavior is called *establishing norms.*

This process is carried out in a uniquely human way. A human being is an animal who can use symbols to picture in his or her mind conditions that do not now exist but that might exist. If we use the verbal symbols of words to say "twelve noon tomorrow," you can imagine all sorts of alternative behaviors you might indulge in at that time. In order to experience then the possible behavior you most prefer, you will start modifying your behavior now. You may phone a friend to join you, borrow money to buy a better lunch, or buy a jar of yogurt on the way home. Human behavior is determined in part not just by the past and the present, but also by a selection of the most preferred future from the array of all possible futures we can imagine. Each individual chooses that one that he or she thinks will be the most worthwhile or rewarding. It is seen as the most valuable, even though the reward may not be immediate.

The very significant way groups control this process of individual choice is by assigning meaning and value to those mental symbols by which we picture the futures. For example, since our society values slimness and yogurt is low in calories, all other things being equal, you may well buy a yogurt for twelve noon tomorrow. The group defines what is "good" or "bad," "right" or "wrong," "beautiful" or "ugly." Through the group's language and picture symbols, the value is conveyed to the individual's mind. That is what establishing norms is all about. The group determines what is "normal" for its members. But this normalcy varies from group to group. The value words have been placed in quotation marks to emphasize the fact that different groups assign different definitions to these words. Humans have no common definitions of those values that encompass all cultures. In fact anthropologists seem to enjoy finding cultures that have the opposite values to those Westerners have defined as "God-given" or "common sense." Is it good to acquire property? An American Indian tribe strives to give it away. Is it acceptable to lay out your living Eskimo grandparents on a melting ice flow? The Chinese could not. Is it good or bad, right or wrong, beautiful or ugly, to have kinky hair?

Culture. All norms woven together comprise a group's *culture*, the unique and particular combination of values and behavior that distinguishes one group from others. Adherence to the culture is a mark of membership in the group. Schools traditionally have been charged with "the transmission of culture" to the new members of society. This particular process of socialization is called *acculturation*, the leading into (Latin, *ad*, which becomes *ac*) the established norms of the society.

However, in order best to cement the group together, an individual must accept these norms as if they were his or her own goals. What will be the most rewarding for the group must at least appear to be most rewarding for the individual. "It's good to go to school because it will help me get a job." That may or may not be true, but it encourages a student who is compelled to attend by law to go more willingly. Members who are new to any group (such as children or immigrants or fraternity pledges) must be trained to believe that behavior the group desires is "normal" behavior. Each member then takes up the goals of the group as his or her *own* goals. They all set themselves "by choice" to the task assigned them by the group, and are able to hold themselves to the desired behavior by a sanction that is intrinsic, that is, within each individual. It seems to the members that any other behavior would be "abnormal." And within the particular group, that is so. This aspect of socialization is called *enculturation*, the establishing of norms in (Latin, *in*, which becomes *en*) the individual.

Socialization, or the establishment of norms, is comprised of both acculturation, which introduces new members to established norms, and enculturation, by which they adopt these norms as their own.

Many factors influence the effectiveness with which these norms are accepted by group members. One of the most potent influences that encourages the adoption of norms is the reward of "a feeling of belonging." Human animals require this support almost as much as they do food and water. Sometimes it is defined as the "affective dimension" of life, the socioemotional component, or simply, "warmth." In order to experience these feelings, human beings will give up much they might otherwise personally prefer. This climate of acceptance is so important that some human groups seem to exist with it, rather than the accomplishing of a mutual task, as a primary goal. Primarily, it isn't the beer and the skittles that bring the local boys to the pub.

The church and the close-knit family have been traditional sources of supports of this sort. With the shriveling of their influence in modern life, many modern persons feel a marked sense of rootlessness and depression. This experience is so common we have a name for it: *alienation*. Many people feel as though they are "aliens" who do not belong in their very own society.

The Relation of These Activities

We have seen how human groups, in order to accomplish the purpose that has brought them into being, must fulfill the functions of (1) decision making, or defining goals; (2) allocation, or assigning roles; (3) integration, or delivering sanctions; and (4) socialization, or establishing norms. These functions can be related to one another in two ways.

One way is to note that the first two functions—defining goals and assigning roles—focus upon the tasks a group must perform, whereas the latter two—delivering sanctions and establishing norms—have more to do with a group's membership. Groups that emphasize decision and allocation, such as corporations or political parties, are frequently characterized as formal groups. Informal groups have a task, but as at a party, integration and socialization are more important.

Another way of perceiving the relationship between these four functions is to note that decision and integration focus on the group as a whole; allocation and socialization focus upon activities of individual members.

These are only emphases, however. Each of the four group functions is concerned to some degree with both the group and individuals, with both the task and the membership. But keep in mind the distinctions we draw here, since they will become important in a later discussion.

THE STRUCTURAL COMPONENTS OF A GROUP

Human beings attempt to understand the world around them. Because they are neither very big nor very fast animals, their survival has depended upon problem solving. If they got into a dangerous situation, they had to figure their way out of it—or should have planned to avoid it in the first place. To improve their understanding, they had to increase their appreciation of how individual facts or data are related to each other and to a whole of which they are parts. The whole gives greater meaning to each part because of that part's particular place in the structure of the whole.

> Here are three dots: ...
> Here they are again: ∴

But are they the same? When you look at the second grouping, you probably respond "triangle." This is an example of your human characteristic of trying to understand by structuring and classifying information coming into your mind. This is what makes you a good solver of problems compared to other animals.

Social scientists studying human behavior in the twentieth century have focused more and more upon studying relationships between the parts and wholes of social structures. Three

British sociologists developed the model in Figure 1.2 from Talcott Parsons' theories of social interaction. (Brian J. Ashley et al., 1971, p. 33)

Figure 1.2 Parsons' Model of Social Interaction

	Instrumental (Means)	Consummatory (Ends)
External	Adaptive Function	Goal Attainment Function
Internal	Pattern Maintenance and Tension Management	Integrative Function

SOURCE: Brian J. Ashley, Harry G. Cohen, and Roy G. Slatter, *An Introduction to the Sociology of Education.* Copyright © 1969 by Brian J. Ashley, Harry G. Cohen, and Roy G. Slatter. Reprinted by permission of Macmillan London and Basingstoke.

In Figure 1.2 you can see four aspects of group life placed in a structural relationship to each other. Parsons used two concepts to make this model: (1) a separation of means (instrumental) and ends (consummatory), and (2) a separation of the internal relationships within the group from those external relationships dealing with other outside groups. Parsons developed this model in the early days of *structuralism*, when this school of thought in the social sciences believed the barriers between parts were important. Early structuralists also viewed ends as separate from means. You can see how Parsons' model reflects these ideas.

In 1969, Ashley, Cohen, and Slatter analyzed the functioning of a school classroom using this model. The adaptive function would use custodial, academic, or crusading means to relate to external forces. Ends were identified with the traditional divisions of education, that is, elementary, preparatory, or developmental. Internal means for maintaining the classroom might be oriented around the teacher, the pupils, or the subject matter; integration achieved by coercive, utilitarian, or normative functions. (Ashley et al., 1971)

The first generation of structuralists, sometimes called *gestaltists* (from the German word for "pattern"), was influenced by concepts from the physical sciences. According to the physics of Isaac Newton, all material things tend to move toward absolute equilibrium or balance between internal and external forces. Hot and cold water, for example, become tepid when mixed. This tendency of a system to move toward equilibrium is called *entropy*.

For the gestaltists, a system that was not moving toward perfect balance, or equilibrium, was not functioning properly. School psychologists and sociologists who were influenced by these ideas used "adjustment" as a key word to express the desired relationship of the child in the classroom and the school within society. Everything was supposed to move toward absolute balance.

However, when this interpretation of behavior was applied to human systems, whether an individual or a group, it caused a good deal of puzzlement. Much data on human behavior simply did not fit the hypothesis of entropy. Few human systems ever attain balance with all the internal and external forces moving upon them. Another explanation was called for.

THE SYSTEM COMPONENTS OF A GROUP

Partially because the original gestaltist structuralist hypotheses of equilibrium and adjustment weren't proving helpful in solving human problems, a new set of concepts developed in the middle third of our century. This time, scholars turned to the biological sciences for a model of human behavior. Preeminent among them was Jean Piaget, a Swiss psychologist who had been trained as a biologist. He developed models of human thought (or cognition) that used biological principles of adaptation to change, namely *assimilation* and *accommodation*. Human beings take in ideas just as cells do food. They absorb them and integrate them into their existing structure, which causes a change in the structure. This process of absorption and reintegration is called assimilation. After there is a change in the system, the organism must change its way of interacting with the surrounding environment. This change in response is the process of accommodation.

At the same time Piaget was developing his revolutionary psychological theories, an anthropologist named Claude Lévi-Strauss attempted to explain human culture in terms of common ideas interacting with various environments. He described, for example, how a tribe's myths are modified when it moves from mountains to plains.

Piaget, Lévi-Strauss, several students of language, and other social scientists became identified with what might be called the "second generation" of structuralists. Essentially, they saw the structures of the earlier thinkers not as static patterns, but rather as dynamic systems—systems that are continually changing and transforming because of the very nature of life itself.

In whatever form life is found, it struggles to avoid perfect equilibrium. A state of perfect rest is death for an organism. So living systems (individuals or groups) may be defined as those systems that by their very nature are *antientropic*. This is precisely what distinguishes organic (and thus human) behavior from purely physical operations. To obtain perfect equilibrium for a living creature is to die—to cease to be. What characterizes living systems is a constant process of transformation, of development, of growth and change—an ongoing effort to overcome the tendency toward entropy. Living systems operate by the same physical laws as other physical systems, so the tendency toward entropy is real. But living systems are also genetically programed to strive to overcome entropy as long as they can.

Piaget calls this process of antientropic interaction with the surroundings equilibration as opposed to equilibrium. *Equilibration* is a process in which the organism moves through a series of constantly changing stages, always passing through a balance point, and always out of balance because it is either in the process of assimilation or accommodation. In a living system, this constant alternation goes on as changes caused by the environment bring about changes in the system (assimilation), which in turn cause changes as the system responds to the environment (accommodation). The process goes on back and forth continuously, with change and transformation characteristic of living behavior up to the very moment of death.

Animals eat (assimilation), which gives them strength to forage in wider circles (accommodation). That effort increases their need for food (assimilation), and so on. Humans read about a new book on Africa (assimilation), which increases their interest in reading more about African animals, which they may have known nothing about before reading the first book (accommodation). Whether interactions are physical or intellectual, living creatures grow and change by the equilibrating processes of assimilation and accommodation.

This new perspective suggests a new way of looking at group behavior. So the newer structuralists speak not of interaction, which focuses upon relationships between parts (the space between the three dots), but upon transformation. This word suggests a change in the *form* of the parts and the whole; in society, it implies a change in the system that encompasses both the group and the individual. Further, structures are no longer defined by inclusion or exclusion, aspects internal and external to them. The boundaries of living macrosystems, like persons and social groups, are as permeable as that microsystem the cell. Effects and influences are viewed as flowing across (Latin, *trans*) what used to be viewed as barriers. So, what we may call *transformational structuralism* interprets human systems as vitally connected with other systems and constantly changing in form due to these connections.

Because process and change occur through time, the passage of time becomes a significant dimension for understanding a system. A true understanding of any human system cannot take place with one quick single look. You need at least two points to chart its line of change and to see the direction of movement. This is why some historical background is included in each chapter of this book. We can know more about today and tomorrow if we have some idea about yesterday.

Function, process, change, time—these are key concepts of the new structuralism that gave rise to this book, *Transforming Schools*. To survive, schools must be vitally connected with the larger human systems of which they are a part, and they must change in form by assimilating and accommodating the effects of those connections.

A TRANSFORMATIONAL MODEL OF A SOCIAL SYSTEM

A transformational model of a social system requires two basic changes from the interaction model in Figure 1.2:

1. In place of a division between means and ends, an emphasis upon the whole group or upon individuals will be substituted. Means flow into ends and are integrally related. They cannot be separated. Nor, of course, can the group or the individuals who make it up be separated. The distinction is only one of emphasis.

2. Transformational structuralism emphasizes the flow of activity between any system and its surrounding systems. A barrier dividing internal from external events is meaningless. Group functions are therefore divided according to whether their emphasis is upon the task dimension or upon the membership dimension. Once again, this is for clarity of emphasis, for each dimension implies the existence of the other.

Figure 1.3 Transformational Model of Social Interaction

	Individual in Focus	Group in Focus
Task	Assigning Roles	Defining Goals
Membership	Establishing Norms	Delivering Sanctions

How does the transformational model of social interaction shown in Figure 1.3 help in understanding a school situation? Suppose you were asked to describe a new form of classroom organization such as the British infants school, or open school, to someone who had been educated solely in the traditional American schoolroom. In a traditional school, the teacher is responsible for defining the goals, allocating which of the children (usually all) will accomplish them, and delivering sanctions to those children who do not conform. A well-liked teacher usually establishes a warm classroom atmosphere of approval that causes a majority of children to accept as their own the norms of behavior she or he establishes. (In fact, if students have strong feelings of support among themselves instead, the ability of the class to perform the goals selected by the teacher may actually be weakened.)

In the open-school setting, the teacher provides a wide variety of goals, or ways for students to meet assigned tasks. Children themselves select or allocate who shall do certain tasks, such as measuring the growth of the class rabbit. The presence of older children as models establishes norms informally by imitation as more children are actively involved in their own learning. The delivery of sanctions is likely to be by fellow students who do not wish their own work interrupted.

In looking at the next level of group organization in education, schools, let us expand the analysis to look at the transformations that take place in one group function when there is a change in another.

For example, traditionally the principal is assigned the role of delivering sanctions. You may have seen that paddle hanging in the principal's office inscribed "The Board of Education." Suppose, however, the school decides to initiate a student court for delivering sanctions to any pupil who needs correction. Suppose at the same time the teachers and pupils assume responsibility for defining the goals, allocating the roles, and setting up norms for performance within each classroom? What happens to the role of the principal? A student court and more teacher responsibility in setting goals suggest a school might do away all together with a "principal" teacher. Of course, he or she still might be needed in order to fill out forms and sort papers.

THE SCHOOL IN THE SOCIAL SYSTEM

The Functions of Social Institutions

If we use the discipline of sociology like a microscope, we can vary the focus from looking at individuals in the roles they each play to looking at the behavior of the group as a whole. We can also enlarge the focus to those multigroup agglomerations we identify as societies, cultures, and nations. The United States is such a system, made up of many subsystems. Within these large societies, group functions are assigned to subsystems, just as in smaller groups special roles are assigned to individual members.

Social institutions are clusters of interlocking roles, whose resulting behavior accomplishes one or more group tasks. For example, the institution of government is charged with the particular task of decision making. The economic system is the social institution assigned to allocate scarce physical and human resources.

Historically, in order to hold society together to make it an integral whole, the institutions of religion and law were responsible for the delivery of sanctions. Today the institutions of the mass media play an almost equally important role in integrating the members of society into a cultural whole.

Finally, the social institution of the school shares with the institution of the family the group task of socialization. So, as we enlarge the focus to an entire society, our model can be expanded to show the relation of the major social institutions to the institution of education, as Figure 1.4 shows.

Figure 1.4 Transformational Model of Society

	Individual in Focus	Group in Focus
Task	Allocation ECONOMIC SYSTEM	Decision Making GOVERNMENTAL PROCESS
Membership	Socialization FAMILY AND SCHOOL	Integration RELIGION, LAW, MASS MEDIA

The operations of social institutions are performed by groups of individuals—government by political parties, for example. While particularly responsible for one function of the supergroup (society), each social institution must of course perform all the group functions within its own sphere. Every political party must allocate, integrate, socialize, and make decisions about how it will perform its special purpose: facilitating the decision-making process in American society.

The Functions of Schools

Are schools fulfilling their task? To answer this, we must look at the tasks society assigns this social institution. Both school and family are expected to establish within the new members of the society three important norms:

1. The knowledge needed for survival of the individual within the society (e.g., the meaning of the symbol of a skull and crossbones on a label)
2. The knowledge needed for the survival of the society itself (e.g., that good Americans don't cheat on their income tax)
3. The desire within each new member to support that society (e.g., recitation of the "Pledge of Allegiance" in class)

Piaget has said that "it happens frequently that a structure changes its function to meet new social needs." (Piaget, 1970, p. 118) What marks the American school system, however, is that while massive changes have occurred in American life, little change has taken place in the schools: the barrier between school and society has been little permeated. We call the failure of schools to assimilate and accommodate social change "educational entropy." There are many examples.

How Schools Have Failed. One glaring example of educational entropy is the schools' failure to adequately assimilate tasks once assigned to religion. The institution of religion, particularly as expressed in formal church structure, originally dominated American education. Religion used to establish goals for our society and deliver sanctions that were awesome. With the lessening of the force of organized religion, however, this institution has little or no direct connection with the public-school system. (Indeed, recent Supreme Court decisions have reemphasized the democratic necessity for the separation of the church from a state-established school.)

Meanwhile, society has transferred to the schools the task of inculcating the values and norms of ethical behavior that were previously a function of pulpit and Sunday School. But there is little evidence that the schools have changed their way of operating to accommodate this new social expectation.

Another example of educational entropy can be found in the failure of schools to respond to the challenge of the mass media. The mass media constitute an extraordinarily powerful new institution for integrating society and socializing its members by means of communication. In previous eras the preferred learned ways of behavior, the culture, were transmitted through family custom, church ritual, and through formal and informal education. Today, the definition of goals and the establishment of norms reaches children in American society more frequently and more insistently through popular songs and TV programs than through all the other nonfamily institutions of society combined.

Because profit-seeking businesses support the mass media in this country, commercial competition determines the values portrayed. For example, TV endlessly broadcasts what the norms and values are expected to be in the relationships between the sexes. The values emphasized are usually physical attractiveness and popularity. This attitude permeates programing as well as commercial messages.

Sociological studies (and common sense) have shown that these values lose their meaning under the stress of extended unemployment of a family breadwinner. But when educators have moved to provide marriage and family life courses that would establish more realistic values, many communities have risen up in arms. Vocal pressure groups have been able to thwart a change that would bring "sex education" into their schools.

Additionally, television may soon surpass the school in teaching the factual information needed for social survival. If schools continue to see dispensing information as their primary function—their *sine qua non*—they may become as superfluous as the principal who neither delivers sanctions nor defines goals.

For failures such as these, many critics of education in America today proclaim, "School is dead." And to the degree that schools have failed to respond to changes in the society around them, have maintained equilibrium and refused to grow, the educational system may indeed be dying as it drifts toward entropy. To cease to change is to die for a human group as surely as for a human individual.

But we hold the belief that the schools can be transformed to developing, ever-renewing human systems. Moreover, we trust that tomorrow's teachers can bring this about. What follows are some specific suggestions. The next four chapters will use the transformational model suggested in Figure 1.4 to analyze the reciprocal role the schools play in relation to the social institutions of government, economics, law and religion, and the family. Chapter 6 and Chapter 7 discuss the school and the classroom, respectively, in terms of social transformation. In conclusion Chapter 8 looks forward to schools of the future.

MAIN IDEAS

1. Groups exist to accomplish purposes individuals cannot accomplish alone.
2. All groups engage in common tasks in order to get their purpose accomplished. These tasks are:
    a. decision making, or defining goals
    b. allocation, or assigning roles
    c. integration, or delivering sanctions
    d. socialization, or establishing norms
3. Establishing norms requires two processes, acculturation and enculturation.
4. Talcott Parsons described group structure using a model based on the ideas of gestaltists, the earliest group of structural sociologists, who emphasized equilibrium.
5. Transformational structuralism holds that living systems are marked by development and change.
    a. Life avoids equilibrium since it implies death, not growth.
    b. Changes in one part of a system cause changes in other parts of the whole system.
    c. As opposed to early static structuralism, transformational structuralism has the dynamic key concepts of function, process, change, and time.
6. A newer model of social process categorizes group processes as focusing upon the group or the individual members and upon the task or the membership functions of the group.
7. Society assigns to specific institutions the various tasks of group functioning.

8. The schools and the family are the social institutions particularly charged with socializing the new members of society.
9. American schools to remain alive must respond to changes in the other institutions of American society.

GLOSSARY

accommodation The biological principle that entities adapt their functions in response to structural change.

acculturation Introduction to the established norms of behavior of society.

alienation The sense of rootlessness and depression that accompanies the experience of not belonging to a cohesive group.

allocation Assigning members to roles within the group.

allocation function The duty of schools to assign students to occupational and other roles in society.

antientropic The tendency for a system, especially a biological one, to avoid perfect equilibrium.

assigned roles Roles with which specific members of a group are charged frequently on the basis of age, sex, or size.

assimilation The biological principle that entities reintegrate their structure by absorption from that which is in their environment.

culture A unique pattern of behavior and values that distinguishes one society from another.

decision making Defining the goals, that is, the means and ends, of a group.

enculturation Adoption of a group's established norms as one's own.

entropy The tendency for a system to approach perfect equilibrium.

equilibration The process in which an organism moves through a series of stages, passing into and out of balance by assimilation and accommodation.

establishing norms The process of defining and inculcating preferred behavior.

gestaltists The first generation of structuralists, who believed that unless systems tend toward equilibrium they are abnormal.

integration Delivering sanctions to protect the group's survival.

peer groups Groups of equals, frequently the same in age, sex, or subculture, who perform a socializing function by encouraging conformity.

roles Group expectations of behavior held in order to accomplish a group task.

sanctions Positive and negative pressures that a group exerts to hold the membership together.

social institutions Subsystems within a society that perform specialized roles.

socialization Establishing norms of behavior for individual members.

socialize To make individuals members of a society.

structuralism The doctrine in social science that examines phenomena in light of relationships between parts and between parts and the whole.

transformational structuralism The doctrine that holds that living systems are vitally connected with other systems and, as a result, are constantly changing in form and function.

BIBLIOGRAPHY

Ashley, Brian J., et al. *An Introduction to the Sociology of Education.* London: Macmillan, 1971.
Buckley, Walter, ed. *Modern Systems Research for the Behavioral Scientist.* Chicago: Aldine, 1968.
Cartwright, Dorwin, and Alvin Zander, eds. *Group Dynamics Research and Theory.* 2nd ed. New York: Harper & Row, 1960.
Gardner, Howard. *The Quest of Mind.* New York: Knopf, 1972.
Piaget, Jean. *Structuralism.* New York: Basic Books, 1970.
Reimer, Everett. *School Is Dead.* Garden City, N.Y.: Doubleday, 1971.

The Schools and Government

	Individual in Focus	Group in Focus
Task		→ Government ← DECISION MAKING → Citizenship ←
Membership		

GOVERNMENT'S ROLE AND ITS RELATION TO EDUCATION

How does a society decide what its goals shall be and the preferred means by which it will reach the goals that are chosen? The system of interrelated activities that accomplishes these functions is called the social institution of government.

Frequently, the word "government" signifies persons such as a governor or a justice of the peace. While people fill these roles in the structure of government, they are not themselves the social institution. Similarly, politics may signify the ward leader, the big city "boss," the volunteer on election day, or, in our country, the political-party system. Seen as social institutions, both politics and government refer to the processes by which decisions are made rather than the persons who are deciding. In a democracy, government involves decision making by *all* citizens. Citizens delegate the responsibility for making some decisions to certain officials. But those officials serve only as representatives of the people who elected them.

Government is the process by which individuals—whether a simple monarch and his court or a democratic legislature and its executive—determine what steps shall be taken to meet the goal of perpetuating the society and the lives of the people within it.

Sometimes the nature of these decisions is the ultimate question of life or death. There may be conflict between the survival of a society and/or the survival of its members. Consider what choices are made when war is declared. This is, of course, the most extreme example. Daily, however, the process of government at all levels results in decisions that affect the lives of the members of the society.

If you think of even the most modern nation as being somewhat like an ancient tribe, you can readily understand how important it is for any society to train its new members in the way that the already established group members wish them to behave. This training of the young is done in order to ensure that the goals the government has decided upon will be carried out even as the old members of the society die away. Since societies change, some of that training must be focused on creativity, on research and development. The consensus of society permits this, if it fosters rather than threatens survival.

As we noted in Chapter 1, schools, although they build on the initial socialization by the family, are the major tool society uses to formally initiate new members into the society. So the two institutions of education and government are closely tied to each other. As a matter of fact, only recently has the development of the student as an individual been seen as a pertinent goal for schooling. The traditional view is that the goals of the public school should be those of the political state that it serves. Questions about whether a course is to be required or elective come from the expectation that society knows best what is "good" for its new members to learn. Usually, required courses fall in the socially needed category. Electives, identified as "frills" by some, may focus more on individual development. Can you report exceptions to this in your own schooling?

In the United States the decision-making function of our society is divided between three levels of government—local, state, and national. The sharing, competition, and coordination of these three separate systems make for some problems peculiar to American schools. Looking at the process of educational decision making at each level—the subject matter of this chapter—illuminates some of the educational conflicts that occur because of the separation between decision-making levels. For example, federal funding for schools was long delayed because of a fear the local school board would lose some of its power to make decisions.

In most European systems only one nationwide department of education oversees the operation of numerous local schools. Flexibility is sacrificed for efficiency and accountability. The specific historical reasons why this pattern is not followed in our society are discussed below.

In the United States the goal-defining function of government is usually handled by a legislative body of elected representatives; an executive branch administers these decisions; and a judicial branch delivers the sanctions of law to enforce them. You probably recognize the President as the Chief Executive of the federal government. Who fulfills this function at the state and local levels? What are the state and local equivalents of Congress? Can you name any of your representatives to these bodies? Knowing the answers to these questions can be important because among the decisions they make are how your taxes will be spent and what salary you will receive as a teacher.

In this chapter the legislative and executive functions will be emphasized. The judicial function of government will be developed more fully in Chapter 4, "Schools and the Integrating Function."

DECISION MAKING AT THE LOCAL LEVEL

History

The form of education in colonial America was much like that
in the mother countries of Europe during the seventeenth and
eighteenth centuries. Most education was in the home, and job
training took place through apprenticeship programs. The
church schools, whether controlled by Protestants or Catholics,
prepared students for university training in the professions of
religion, law, and medicine. In some locales dame schools provided training in the "three Rs" for those students whose parents could afford the luxury of hiring a local woman to complete the parental task of education.

After American independence, the establishment of a democratic form of government required an educated electorate.
Thomas Jefferson expressed this concern in saying:

> I know of no safe depository of the ultimate powers of society
> but the people themselves, and if we think them not enlightened
> enough to exercise their control with a wholesome discretion,
> the remedy is not to take it from them, but to inform their
> discretion by education. (Letter to William C. Jarvis, 9 September
> 1820; quoted in Gordon C. Lee, 1961, p. 17)

Within fifty years, so-called common schools for learning
that which was needed in common by all potential voters were
established to provide the fundamentals of literacy and basic
arithmetic for the citizens and artisans of the new land.

These common schools were overseen by local persons not
only because of a geographic necessity (mass communication
and transportation were still things of the future) but also because the Founding Fathers were deeply concerned about a too
powerful central government. They realized that a national
state tending toward tyranny could solidify its control over the
people by manipulating the education they received in the established schools. The preference for local control of the
schools, therefore, has a long and deep tradition in our country.
Local control derives its power specifically from a fear of totali-
tarianism and its role from a concern to prevent the perversion

of democracy. As recently as 1974 a Supreme Court decision *(Bradley* v. *Milliken)* reaffirmed this principle of local control of public schools. Implementing this principle there are thousands of local school boards throughout the country, which are primarily responsible for all decisions affecting schools in their districts.

What Do Local School Boards Decide?

There are variations in the power of local school boards, but most school boards make decisions concerning the following important facets of public education:

1. Who shall teach—by hiring and firing staff
2. What shall be taught—by controlling the scope and sequence of instruction
3. How shall the money be divided among the school's needs—by developing the budget
4. How shall the money be raised—by levying taxes and borrowing funds

The board is also charged with maintaining the extensive property and equipment of a modern school system. Even in a small district, this "plant," as it is called, may be worth millions of dollars.

These are important tasks—tasks that directly and decisively affect what happens in the classroom, what a teacher can and cannot do. Seldom, however, do teachers serve on school boards. Some districts actually prohibit teachers, who are employees, from sitting on boards that employ them. But teachers seldom seek board positions, even when no regulation prevents it. An interesting question you might pursue on your own is why this might be so. We will turn now to the questions of the structure and workings of the school board.

How Are School Boards Chosen?

Distrust of political manipulation, as we saw, led to a preference for local, rather than national, control of the school. In a further attempt to remove schools and the persons who make the decisions for them from the influences of politics, school-board members sometimes are appointed rather than elected. Unless terms are long and staggered, however, appointments may lead to even greater control by the political party that has the power to appoint.

Some school boards, therefore, are elected, but at times other than when general elections are held. The problem with this technique is that it discourages the participation of voters who might come out only at the time of a general election. Furthermore, although candidates frequently run with no political affiliation, parties may move behind the scenes to control them, resulting in a more pernicious situation than if party affiliation and accountability were clearly announced.

Clearly, no method is without its dangers and advantages, and each presupposes the active participation of an interested electorate. But appearance at the polling booth is not guaranteed in our society. Indeed, many school-board elections bring out fewer voters than there are teachers in a system. Even many teachers fail to vote for those who will make decisions that affect their wages and working conditions.

Who Serves on School Boards?

The reasons individuals run for a school board—a job that is seldom paid and requires hours of exhaustive labor—vary. In some localities, the political implications of school-board decision making attract young persons who see this service as the first step up the political ladder.

Other candidates appear to serve simply out of a sense of civic duty, for the better working of the democratic system, or for some personal reward of public or individual recognition. Americans are world-renowned for their habit of devoting hours of effort to community causes, and foremost are the thousands of men and women across America who voluntarily labor for our schools on hundreds of local boards of education.

Generally, the board members who are not politically motivated are professional people and members of the community who wish to maintain the status quo—things as they are. These might include established business people, retired professionals, and civic-minded homemakers. In general board members are from the upper-middle or lower-upper social classes. This group naturally has no wish to radically transform the schools (or society through the schools), for they usually hold a preferred place within that society. Board membership is infrequently sought by persons who represent dissatisfied special-interest groups or ethnic minorities.

When a change-oriented person attains a rare position on a board, his or her views may be lost, since holdovers serving overlapping terms may tend to block rapid or radical change in the course of school policy they have previously supported.

What Neighborhood Is Local?

The establishment of local school boards would seem to encourage community participation, but currently the question of what constitutes a locality has been raised. In the nineteenth century, some American communities grew and expanded into the massive urban centers that are now the home of most American school-children. The "local" board has become far removed from the neighborhood children that it was established to serve. The recent history of education in urban areas has been marked by an attempt at renewed community control. Because of housing patterns, however, these smaller communities (within the massive city school districts) are frequently ethnically homogeneous. Almost all the families are similar in cultural or economic background. So the advantages of returning control to the parents and local citizens closest to the school may be counterbalanced by withdrawing into schools that are racially, culturally, and economically homogeneous. Thus, the educational system is prevented from playing its traditionally assigned role in America: an integrator into the cultural melting pot. (Sandra Feldman, 1968) Some critics say the prevalence of neighborhood schools in big-city systems prevented cultural assimilation anyway. And perhaps we should prefer cultural diversity if the result of the melting simply brought white Anglo-Saxon dominance over other cultures.

The question of how local is local, that is, how large a school system ought to be in order to have its own board, has not been determined and is one of the liveliest issues in urban education today. There does seem to be evidence that the more control parents are able to have upon the decisions made about the school, the better the achievement of the children in the school. (Carol Lopate et al., 1969) Parent involvement affecting pupil achievement is a good example of the transforming effect upon one aspect of a system that occurs when change happens in another part of the system. How could you explain this by using the transformational model in Figure 1.4?

What Influences the Boards' Decisions?

As related above, the decision-making process of the local school board is affected by the economic and personal history of its members. Decisions are also a result of the shifting alignment of competing forces of influential community groups. These groups include the economic establishment of the community, the PTA, a local union, and more recently the teachers' organization. If the establishment wants lower taxes, and the teachers higher wages, what decision is made? Of course, some boards occupy their time with less pressing matters, such as which synthetic fiber should be used for school carpeting. And some scholars believe that in actuality school boards do little but give legal sanction to policies made by the school administration.

Whether a board does take part in significant decision making depends upon the size of the community the board represents, whether the district is rural or urban, and whether members are elected or appointed. Further variations occur in the members real power to make decisions as a result of particular patterns of multiple community groups that may be allied to get some measure they prefer accepted. A solid, broad-based citizens' coalition can sway the most entrenched board.

But, what seems to be the most consistent influential factor in educational decision making is the relative autonomy or independence of the educational establishment, the school administrative structure itself. (Paul E. Peterson, 1974)

The Superintendent's Role. The school board acts as a legislature (and a jury) for the school districts. The chief executive of the system is the superintendent. He or she is the individual charged with administering the policies of the board (frequently serving as the ex officio secretary of the board). What board members decide, the superintendent is expected to carry out. If they define a curriculum change, he or she has to set in motion the process of buying materials and retraining teachers. If a new building is called for, the chief executive interviews architects. Of course, in a large system, the superintendent will delegate many of these specific chores to an administrative staff. But the power to delegate and the ultimate responsibility for fulfilling the board's wishes is the superintendent's.

A more hidden but equally powerful influence of the superintendent upon the board flows from the board's need for background information in making decisions. As the chief school officer, the superintendent is expected to act as a guide to the board's decisions by marshaling the facts to be presented. Since few board members have more than a layman's knowledge of educational theory or practice, the control of the superintendent to filter information that the board receives tends to give the chief executive great power in their decision-making process. For example, teacher candidates who appeal to and are proposed by the superintendent are usually appointed by the board without question.

The superintendent brings not only professional expertise to the board, but also a perception of public opinion in the community. Through contact with various community opinion makers, he or she ought to be in a position to guide the board to decisions the public will accept, and away from those the public will reject. The 1974 textbook controversy in a West Virginia county placed the superintendent in the position of continuing the local board's policy while attempting to marshal majority support against a highly vocal minority in opposition to the board. A superintendent's leadership ability is therefore as decisive in meetings of the board as it is in a district-wide teachers' conference. Sometimes a superintendent who has great political influence with a board may appear deceptively ineffectual in a meeting with teachers. He or she may indeed simply know and practice where it is most significant to exert a power thrust. The superintendent must keep the board's support in order to achieve hoped for goals. To lose that support is the last step before losing the position of superintendent.

Ascribed and Achieved Roles. A school board, like any other group, assigns roles to its members. Generally, there is an elected president with the *ascribed role* of leader. That is to say, the role he or she plays is formally defined and allocated by the group. Frequently, as in other groups, the leadership function is shared, or even taken over, by another member of the group, and that role is described sociologically as the *achieved role* of leader. A talent for leadership will generally bring a member a leader's actual tasks—regardless of whether he or she bears the ascribed title. Groups appear to function most smoothly when the same individual is both the achieved and ascribed leader.

The superintendent and the board president may display reciprocity or rivalry in leadership. Each has a portion of ascribed leadership. Each may strive to achieve more. Without a usually harmonious relationship between the superintendent and the board, the school system suffers from lack of clear direction and focus in decision making. New curricula the superintendent wants introduced may be prohibited by a board or so underfunded that they fail. Curricula the board wants must also have the superintendent's support. Neither segment of district decision making can move too far in front of the other.

Bureaucracy. As the size of the school system increases, the board and the superintendent must delegate more decisions to other educational administrators. The more size, the more delegation, and so on, the decisions trickle down through layers of administrators to a school's principal. The structure of school systems in America today matches the structure of other large businesses and is frequently characterized by the word *bureaucracy.* In order to understand this administrative influence upon the decisions of a board and the superintendent, it is necessary to have some understanding of how the bureaucratic process operates.

The origins of bureaucracy can be found in the Industrial Revolution, which created a need to control the actions of human beings in their interactions with machines. Bureaucratic organization is an attempt to standardize the behavior of persons in a system so that their operations mesh with the operations of machines into a smooth flow of interchangeable parts and activities. The workers on the second shift must show up promptly to ensure that the motors continue to settle down on the chasses as the automobiles move along the assembly line. No matter who does the job (any job), the same job must get done.

With the introduction of huge, complex, and expensive machinery, it became necessary to have workers who could feed raw materials to the machines, work with them in the manufacturing process, and remove the finished products with maximum efficiency. A faulty employee might cause the assembly line to shut down or a valuable and expensive machine to fail. Humans had to be as interchangeable as any other part of the assembly line, and the work accomplished reliably no matter who filled the role of worker.

At a step back from the machinery, paper work had to flow smoothly to make sure the raw materials arrived on time. Decisions had to be made to procure these particular materials rather than others that would be less efficient for the whole process. The entire human part of the production scheme has increasingly been regulated by the demands of the machines with which people share the job of production.

In order to assure human functioning to match the machines' functioning, three characteristics now dominate much of the working behavior of most Americans:

1. Work rules are closely defined (e.g., work begins promptly at nine).
2. Skills are specialized (e.g., unions forbid machinists to do electricians' work).
3. A tight set of rules regulates the conduct of whoever holds a certain position (e.g., foremen must eat in the supervisors' cafeteria).

To speed the flow of decision making, most work positions are arranged in a rigid hierarchy (like drawers in a *bureau*), with many workers taking orders from a foreman, fewer foremen taking orders from a plant manager, and so on up to the board of directors. If humans adhere to these rules, their work should mesh with machines. Bureaucratic operations can be very efficient. Little time is wasted figuring out who ought to do what or when. The system automatically answers those questions. Efficiency has long been valued as a "good" in American society.

Bureaucratic decision making is also characterized by the use of reason and logic—as opposed to an appeal to emotions or ties of kinship or friendship. The structured procedures of logical analysis permit bureaucratic organizations to utilize computers now in many of their decision-making procedures. Terms developed for computers are found in many discussions about educational planning whether or not the machines are actually being used. The glossary of this chapter contains a list of these terms with which modern educators should be familiar.

Computers operate according to *programs* that humans develop. Programing creates a *flowchart* of sequential questions and orders to the computer that enable it to sort the *bits* of information *(data bank)* available to it in its storage unit *(memory bank)* or new data *(input)*, in order to produce the answers *(output)* to problems posed by the human questioner. Typical questions a computer can answer include:

What basic skill weaknesses are indicated by John's answers on his computer assisted mathematics instruction?

What effect would raising school taxes have on the property values of this district?

One of the most essential concepts of the communication theory used with computers is that of *feedback.* At various decision *(branch)* points in the program, knowledge of results obtained so far is fed back to the computer, which permits a change in the direction of the decision-making process toward greater accuracy of results. These are decision points on the flowchart. Ideally, test results should fulfill the same function for students.

Interfacing with machines is central to any technological society like that of the United States today. As a result other characteristics of bureaucracy such as specialization, rigid role expectations, and hierarchical decision making have also been adopted in our culture as values that are "good" in and for themselves. The cultural revolution of the 1960s was essentially a challenge to these values.

Possible changes in the future requirements of industry may encourage societies to abandon bureaucracy as a method of organization of human behavior. In industry, miniaturization (as in solid state transistors) and computerization, which relieves man of much decision making, may change the behaviors needed for the production of goods. This is one change to be considered in the final chapter, "Transformation for Tomorrow." As to bureaucracy in schools, many scholars are beginning to question whether learning and bureaucracy are really compatible. We will explore specific challenges to the assumption that schools must pattern themselves on the bureaucratic structures and values of society at large in Chapter 6.

The fact remains, however, that bureaucratic methods are to be found in most public schools today—to the detriment of needed change. You can see bureaucracy operating in schools in the following ways:

1. A bureaucratic hierarchy is present in the organization of American schools, with workers (students) taking orders from the foreman (teacher), who reports to the plant manager (principal) and so on up to the board of education.
2. Student and teacher handbooks spell out the role expectations of the lower strata in bureaucracy. Who has power over whom is clearly identified.
3. Increasing specialization removes the "principal teacher" out of a teachers' organization and into an association of his fellow administrators.

Indeed, so many decisions are made automatically by the rules and expectations of a bureaucratic system that some educators wonder if we can have freedom at all within our educational system. (*Freedom, Bureaucracy, and Schooling,* 1971) How many times when you were going through school did you receive the response, "No, you can't. It's against the rules," as reason enough for refusal?

Although the superintendent is at the peak of the bureaucratic pyramid and appears all powerful, his or her wishes are controlled by the regulations that govern the other members of the system. Some of these regulations, such as the number of teachers allowed in proportion to the number of students, are defined by legal statute. The superintendent is also controlled by the increasing specialization of staff members. The chief executive may wish to introduce a new course but be unable to find a "certified" teacher to teach it.

Teacher certification and student-teacher ratios are usually regulated by the second level of political control in education—the state.

DECISION MAKING AT THE STATE LEVEL

History

Many court decisions have established that the state governments have the ultimate power for education in our country. The basis for these decisions is constitutional. Since mention of education was *excluded* from the federal Constitution, it is among those powers reserved to the people or the states. The federal government has only those powers specifically delegated to it in the Constitution.

As American culture grew in complexity throughout the nineteenth century, compulsory education for all citizens (whether or not they were franchised) became more widespread. By the beginning of the twentieth century, all children across America were required by their individual state legislatures to attend school. A locality no longer had the choice of whether or not to establish a school. The state could create a school system and then delegate its actual functioning to a local board.

The increase in the number of schools and the number of students required to attend them created problems that appeared to go beyond the power of local boards to solve:

1. Competent teachers had to be identified and certified as competent.
2. Taxes had to be raised statewide to support schools in poor districts.

3. Attendance of millions of children had to be taken to ensure they were in school.
4. A statewide school board was needed to advise the decision makers of the state legislature.

States moved to select statewide boards of education and chief school officers for the state. Not surprisingly, the methods developed on the local level were expanded to the state. So the selection of state boards of education and the state chief school officer parallels the methods of selecting local boards and superintendents. Their social and economic backgrounds also are similar to those of local board members. State boards therefore have the same strengths and weaknesses described for local boards.

The Functions of State Departments of Education

Central statewide departments of public instruction were established to see to the distribution of tax monies and recording of public attendance. These two functions were tied together because attendance "earned" the state's monetary aid to local districts. Minimum criteria were established for obtaining a license as a teacher. A teacher's credentials were collected and examined to see whether the individual could be certified as a licensed teacher. As the years passed, myriad papers had to be filled out to make sure all these regulations of taxes, attendance, and certification were being met.

Today the central function of the state education division is overseeing regulations of public schools. The departments are concerned with teacher certification, school-leaving age, compilation of credits toward graduation, and building construction. They are also frequently responsible for such auxiliary services as cafeterias and bus transportation. All the reports on these activities create a rich source of information about various school functions. In order to mine this lode, many state education departments also have a research department. It is responsible for identifying better school programs by analyzing statistics drawn from this data base.

A major responsibility of state departments is the allocation of tax monies to equalize the financial resources among school systems. Local districts differ widely in taxable wealth, but children are believed to have a right to equal educational opportunity. Since equalization is directly related to the economic function of the schools and society, we will postpone a discussion of it to Chapter 3.

The Relation of State and Local Levels

Local districts and their administrative hierarchies exist at the pleasure of the state and may be consolidated or divided, created or abolished at the will of the state legislature. This dual responsibility can cause difficulties. Claiming a 1968 state-directed consolidation had legally segregated city schools, the Wilmington (Delaware) School Board sued the state board to facilitate federally court-ordered desegregation.

In general, however, since the immediate tasks of educating children are delegated by the state to the local school districts, state departments of education have little direct control over school-children. Also, the same bureaucratic restraints that operate upon each local administration restrict the state decision makers as well. And, of course, a local board may also utilize delaying or modifying tactics to blunt the force of a state directive.

But the classroom situation is affected by the long-range impact of tax policies and changes in statute regulations regarding attendance, class size, and certification. The power of the state legislature over what happens in a schoolroom is therefore decisive if distant. Only recently have teachers organized politically in order to influence the decisions of the state legislators.

DECISION MAKING AT THE NATIONAL LEVEL

History

If you study Table 2.1, which lists the important dates of federal action in the field of education, you will perceive some of the significant trends in that history. Note, for example, the

TABLE 2.1 IMPORTANT FEDERAL DECISIONS ON EDUCATION

Date	Legislation or Decision	Effect
1785	Northwest Ordinance	Requires land to be set aside for institutions of higher learning
*1819	Dartmouth College Case	Makes a private college charter immune to changes by a state legislature
1862	Morrill Act	Establishes land grant colleges for education in agriculture, mining, and home economics
1867	Act to Establish an Office of Education	Establishes the U.S. Office of Education (USOE) for research and development
1890	Second Morrill Act	Gives financial grants to institutions of higher learning with agricultural courses, etc.
*1896	Plessy v. Ferguson	Allows "separate but equal" schools as constitutional
1917	Smith-Hughes Act	Sets up vocational education in high schools
1935	Act to Emend the Agricultural Adjustment Act	Establishes school lunch program
1937	George-Dean Act	Sets up distributive (merchandising) education in high schools
1944	G.I. Bill of Rights	Permits veterans a free education
1950	National Science Foundation Act	Sets up research and improvement of science education
*1952	Zorach v. Clausen	Allows released time for religious education
*1954	Brown v. the Board of Education of Topeka, Kansas	Declares schools segregated by law unconstitutional
1958	National Defense Education Act (NDEA)	Supports science, guidance, foreign language, audio-visual aids
*1962	Murray v. Curlett	Prohibits established religious exercises in public schools

*Supreme Court decisions. Others are legislation.

TABLE 2.1 IMPORTANT FEDERAL DECISIONS ON EDUCATION

1962 Manpower Development Act	Establishes vocational training and retraining outside of public schools
1963 Higher Educational Facilities Act	Supports college construction costs
1964 Civil Rights Act	Grants federal aid for desegregating systems
1965 Elementary and Secondary Education Act (ESEA)	Allows direct federal aid to public- and private-school students
1965 Second Higher Education Act	Grants federal aid directly to colleges
1965 National Foundation on the Arts and Humanities Act	Supports arts and humanities
*1969 *Tinker* v. *Des Moines Independent Community School District*	Extends constitutional rights to students
*1971 *Earle* v. *Dicenso*	Declares aid to parochial schools unconstitutional
*1971 *Swann* v. *Charlottesville-Mecklenburg Board of Education*	Declares busing to bring about desegregation constitutional
1972 Educational Amendment Act	Transforms USOE into the National Institute of Education (NIE) for greater emphasis on research and development and prevents discrimination by sex
*1974 *Milliken* v. *Bradley*	Declares local control is primary to racial desegregation

*Supreme Court decisions. Others are legislation.

dates themselves. There is only one in the eighteenth century, five in the nineteenth, five in the first half of the twentieth century, and sixteen in the third quarter. During that time the nation has been drawn together through mass communication and transportation. Industrial production has demanded an increasingly complex web of acquisition of materials and distribution of products. The needs of our national society have taken precedence over the demands of local needs. Naturally, the needs of education have been enlarged to match the size of the growing dimensions of social interaction.

Most recently the federal government has moved widely into the field of education because of the nation's interaction with other countries. When the Soviet Union launched the first space satellite, a paroxysm of concern convulsed the United States and the Congress. Why had we "fallen behind"? The National Defense Education Act (NDEA) sped federal money to local districts to support curricula and services that would help the United States to "catch up."

All the branches of the federal government have a wide impact on local schools. Recently, decisions of the Supreme Court have been particularly significant to educators. But we will defer discussion of the court's impact until Chapter 4, where we take up the relation of the schools to the law. Here we will concentrate on the influence of other federal policies and programs on education. As you read, try to see what progression of concerns and goals there is in the increasing amount of federal legislation affecting schools.

Activities of the Federal Government as Educator

The primary power that the national government has over education is in the allocation of funds. Federal monies usually are allocated to and spent by state and local districts. The old fear of tyranny of the Founding Fathers is still evident in this attempt to limit the direct control of the federal government upon school-children. The very availability of federal funds for one purpose rather than another, however, all but guarantees the choice of that purpose by local decision makers. A characteristic example of this tendency was the sudden upswing in the status and amount of science in the curriculum of the schools following the 1958 passage of the National Defense Education Act.

In addition to the power of the federal government to control education through the selective allocation of monies, the national government also ranks as the second largest educational establishment through its various programs in the Department of Defense. Since one of America's goals appears to be national survival through force of arms, more persons are educated in military skills than in all other vocational programs combined. This is especially so when a military draft is in operation. As all the recruiting posters tell us, training in military skills may also have some carry-over into civilian occupations. So for some citizens, the armed forces are the vocational capstone upon the general education they have received in the public school.

Paradoxically, the federal government also maintains the most segregated school system in the country. The Department of the Interior purports to serve the needs of native Americans through its special Bureau of Indian Affairs schools.

Inconsistencies like this last example suggest that the role of the federal government does not follow a cohesive, rational, or integrated program in establishing goals for the American schoolchild. In most other industrialized countries, a powerful central government bureau carries out a clear set of established goals. The halting, vacillating efforts of the Congress show that our federal program is more likely to react to the pressures of special-interest groups and various clusters of claimants for national support than to follow a straight line to a defined goal. Public policy instead derives by fits and starts from the successive pressures of needful groups that influence the Congress, or from pressures that arise when a "clear and present" danger is sensed, as in the case of the National Defense Education Act.

Clearly, both industry and labor stand to benefit from monies spent on vocational education, so this sort of legislation has passed easily. However, monies to be spent more generally for all elementary and secondary schools were delayed a decade because of the pressure of the National Educational Association (NEA), an organization of public-school teachers. The NEA feared that money spent on children enrolled in parochial schools would weaken the near monopoly of public education and so, naturally, weaken the power of any organization of public-school teachers. It took the nation ten years to reach a compromise so that children might be aided regardless of where they attended school. This compromise is discussed in Chapter 4.

The National Institute of Education

An Office of Education was established in 1867 to keep national records of records kept by the states. These data could provide a picture of the condition of education nationwide. A 1972 revision changed this bureau into the National Institute of Education (NIE), thereby emphasizing its research and development functions. The NIE bureaucracy, which makes up nearly 20,000 of the 112,000 workers in the Department of Health, Education, and Welfare, exists in an essentially supportive role to the state and local school systems. Public policy is not expected to issue from this agency because the danger of federal control is still feared. But the traditional desire to limit the determination of educational policy by the federal government is now in dynamic tension with the need to fulfill nationwide goals in the areas of defense, ecology, and better manpower utilization. And if we look at the momentum and pattern of federal legislation, it seems that the direction of change is toward increasing federal control.

THE IMPACT OF SCHOOLS UPON DECISION MAKING AND GOVERNMENT

Public support of schools for all citizens arose in response to the democratic need for an educated electorate. If the people are to decide, or at least to elect those who will decide for the whole, then each member of society needs to make the best decision possible on behalf of all others. Thomas Jefferson saw that clearly.

In the first years of this republic, it was believed that an education in literacy would guarantee proper decision making. It would be supported by a free press that could bring the issues to the masses of the electorate. Schools, therefore, supported the decision-making function of society almost exclusively by training in literacy. The curriculum of eighteenth-century schools was heavily influenced by the classical tradition of the European Enlightenment. So physical science might find a place in the curriculum, but political science was not yet deemed a worthy academic study. (The classical Greeks, incidentally, were certain that both were needed in the education of free men.)

Then, as masses of immigrants began to flood into the new cities in the nineteenth century, it appeared that beyond literacy, what was required was a reeducation of those new citizens. Some came from European and Asian kingdoms and empires. Some came from slavery in the United States. Few had learned decision making by community participation in town meetings and myriad other social organizations. To make up for this lack of democratic experience, courses in American history and civics were introduced into the curriculum of the schools.

These courses were considered so important that American history was scheduled for the end of the elementary school to "catch" any who might not continue through grammar school. At the end of grammar school, American history was required so high-school drop-outs did not miss it; and finally, most senior high-school students were submitted to a third year of national history. Not surprisingly, many of them felt they had "had it" by then.

The twentieth century brought to the fore John Dewey's influential vision of the interrelationship of schools and society. The publication of his book *Schools and Society* in 1915 was followed by the social upheaval of economic depression in the 1930s. The impact of Dewey's theory and economic reality led schools to add courses in problems of democracy (POD) as a supplement to history classes. POD classes were sometimes taught using the student project, learn-by-doing methods advocated by the philosopher-psychologist Dewey. Frequently, however, POD was taught via lecture and textbook in the same style as traditional American history classes. School personnel apparently thought they were following proper procedures in citizenship education for there has been little change in the long and established tradition of these social studies curricula.

What has been your experience in this field? Did your school inspire you to be an enlightened and participating voter or officeholder?

Citizenship Education in Practice

A poll taken at the request of the Senate Subcommittee on Intergovernmental Relations in 1973 (and reported in *Newsweek*, 10 December 1973) indicated that while 73 percent said they had voted in the 1972 presidential election, only

- 55 percent actually had.
- 56 percent claimed they had voted on a school-board issue.
- 46 percent could name their representative to Congress.
- 38 percent did not know that the Congress is composed of the Senate and House of Representatives.
- 33 percent claimed to have ever written to their congressional representative.
- 14 percent had worked or actively campaigned for a political candidate.

These figures suggest that American school systems have failed spectacularly in creating responsible citizens—the primary task for which they were established. By default, decision makers are elected by those who have special interests. Naturally, this results in policy making by pressure rather than purpose.

It appears that the schools have not failed solely by default. Not only have they *not* done the assigned task, they have actually taught students *not* to be decision makers. Clear lessons, by example and precept, are laid out in the classroom—but their impact is to repress whatever urgings toward active decision making youth may have. Innumerable psychological studies show that information alone is rarely enough to cause a change in behavior. Schools may provide many social studies facts ("how a bill becomes a law") but have rarely provided those experiences that would encourage students to establish and maintain habits of good citizenship.

If one assumes teachers know best what cultural facts should be transmitted, students will make few decisions concerning their methods of learning or choice of subject matter. Little or no opportunity need be provided within the academic day for students to evaluate for themselves the outcome of their few available choices. Even the grading of work done at the teacher's direction, when it is reduced to a letter or number, is bled of any significant information that might help in evaluating decisions about amount and depth of studying that led to the grade.

Guidance counselors may be available, but they usually have so many student-clients that each one only has a few moments of mutual consideration of a future vocational choice. If a student's behavior has been radically against the established goals of the school, he or she may get some chance to evaluate past decisions with a counselor. Otherwise, there is usually no time in the guidance interview for in-depth consideration of past or present choices.

Opportunities to test out various choices in either academic or extracurricular areas are frequently canceled by restrictive entrance requirements into courses or activities. It is hard to sign up for Algebra I in ninth grade knowing that failure will cast a shadow on college entrance three years later.

How would you evaluate the "student government" at the school you attended? Most graduates report it was an insulated experience for a selected group of school "leaders." A sense of powerlessness in making choices, no lessons in learning how to choose, and no opportunity to evaluate choice have been the training diet of many democratic citizens.

Schools charged with preparing youth for participation as citizens have, apparently, prepared them to drift helplessly under decisions made by pressures from special-interest groups. When adults make all the real decisions in school, it's easy to believe "they" (someone else) make decisions out of school. The same poll quoted above found that over 60 percent felt "what you think doesn't count much any more," and 50 percent felt "people running the country don't really care what happens to you."

The number of possible courses of action, the number of decisions that will need to be made will increase radically in the twenty-first century. If our democracy is to survive, no area of schooling is more in need of transformation. Learning how to decide is an essential skill for tomorrow's citizens. This means first that each teacher must emphasize choosing wisely as one of the most important skills to be learned. Secondly, schools must make a 180° turn from the present practice of discouraging decision making to an attitude that sees school experience as a laboratory for a series of considered and evaluated choices.

MAIN IDEAS

1. Government is the social institution most concerned with the processes of defining goals and decision making.
2. Local control of American schools is based on a desire to keep them free from a single strong national dictation.
3. Local school boards approve many of the most significant and important decisions affecting teaching and learning.
4. School-board members and their decisions tend to protect the status quo.
5. Leadership is provided to the local school board by the superintendent or chief school officer.
6. With the Industrial Revolution, bureaucracy—a system of organizing human behavior to mesh with the manufacturing process—arose.
7. School systems exhibit bureaucratic organization that is common to all technological societies.
8. Control of education by the states is guaranteed in the federal Constitution. Except for the establishment and monitoring of requirements and regulations, most power is delegated to local systems.
9. Federal involvement with education has grown with the national intertwining of our economic system and the desire to keep up with other nations.
10. The federal government, by allocating massive amounts of funds, is able to support programs in the national interest.
11. Through the Department of Defense and the Bureau of Indian Affairs, the federal government is directly involved in operating schools.
12. Homogenization of national culture and problems indicates future increase in federal pressure upon local and state boards of education to conform to one common set of educational goals.
13. The citizenship education for which, in theory, schools re-

ceive public funds appears not to exist in practice. Schools have, in fact, taught students to avoid decision making.

14. To avoid future decisions falling into the hands of pressure groups and special interests, schools must completely revise their procedures in order to help students "learn how to decide."

GLOSSARY

achieved role   A role taken over by a member on the basis of success at some group task.

ascribed role   A formally assigned and allocated role.

bureaucracy   An organization of a group characterized by rules of work that are closely defined, roles based on specialized skills and arranged in a layered or hierarchical structure.

common schools   Early public schools in the United States.

government   The process by which individuals determine what steps will be taken to meet the goal of perpetuating the society and the lives of the people within it.

Common Terms from Computer Science

bits   Single units or items of information, constellations of which, such as name (1 bit), age (1 bit), sex (1 bit), class rank (1 bit), may be used to describe a system unit, such as a student. Bits must be based on mathematic description.

branch (branching)   Choice among alternate possible program sequences on an overall flowchart.

data bank   Information described in bits available to the computer in decision making.

feedback   Knowledge of results so far entered into a program. Feedback influences which branch of subsequent paths on the flowchart will be followed.

flowchart   The sequential system of procedures and check points that describe the flow of information from raw input to final output results.

input All information—both bits and programs—entered into a computer. This information must be able to be expressed mathematically (quantitatively) in order to be entered.

memory bank Information stored on a short- or long-term basis in a computer and available for use.

output Quantitative statements describing the results of a computer's applying a program to data provided to it. (Because the quality of the input determines the quality of the output, criticism of the results of computer use is sometimes expressed: "Garbage in, garbage out.")

programs (programing) Instructions in the form of questions and orders to a computer enabling it to transform unstructured information into a form meaningful to humans.

SUGGESTED ACTIVITIES

Below and after each of the remaining chapters are suggestions for some activities you might engage in alone, with other classmates, or perhaps as a whole class. Undoubtedly you had some ideas for investigation as you read this chapter. Since these ideas are interesting to you, they are probably at least as worthwhile as those on this list. Do not feel limited to what is suggested here.

General Suggestions

1. Prepare yourself for interviews and invited visitors to the class by reading in the files of local newspapers to see what has been going on previous to the meeting you attend. Try to get copies of meeting agendas beforehand. Biographies of meeting members are helpful for showing individual differences to which you should be sensitive. Take notes on the processes as well as the content of meetings. (A technique for charting group processes can be found in Chapter 7.) Discuss with your classmates what you and they have observed. Try to analyze what you observe, to understand it in greater depth because of your reading and any comparison you might make with other activities and with the perspectives of your peers.

2. Surveys and questionnaires, in order to have any scientific validity, require a great deal of time and care, including sophisticated statistical techniques. It is probable that both the number of persons you can interview and the skill with which you can now analyze your results are far too limited to put much faith in how true a measure you have taken of reality. Nevertheless, such surveys and questionnaires may suggest some interesting ideas for further study—and acquaint you with the difficulties of this sort of scientific procedure.

Specific Suggestions

1. Visit one or more meetings of the decision-making groups listed below, and observe their activities.

   a. A school board. (Large school districts may have public relations officers who will assist you in getting the background information. The superintendent's secretary may be a good source in a smaller district.)

   b. The trustees or board of a private, free, or parochial school. (You may want to compare the concerns and decision-making process of a nonpublic school with a public school board.)

   c. Your state legislature's education committee. (If these meetings are closed to the public, you have a good incentive to exert political pressure to pass a state "Right to Know" law.)

   d. One or more student councils.

Before the meeting or while observing the proceedings, you may want to find out:

   a. Who holds ascribed and achieved leadership roles?

   b. How do patterns of communication reflect the status and power of individual group members?

   c. Are decisions debated in the public meeting or do they appear to be rubber-stamped following closed deliberations?

    d. Are citizens' groups active? How do they vary in visibility, organization, and apparent power to influence decisions?

    e. How does the observed group fulfill its membership as well as task functions?

2. Invite a school finance officer to explain how decisions were reached in making up the budget.

3. Simulate a board meeting focusing on a decision that must be made. Perhaps a teacher is proposing an innovative social studies curriculum. How does this technique sensitize you to the importance of the membership functions in group interaction?

4. Interview a cross-section of the public about changes they would like to see made in the schools, and how they believe they might be able to get these changes made.

5. Observe a student council election, noting the appeals of the candidates and the involvement of the rest of the student body.

BIBLIOGRAPHY

Boocock, Sarane S. *An Introduction to the Sociology of Learning.* Boston: Houghton Mifflin, 1972. (See especially Chapter 12, "The Community and the School Board.")

Feldman, Sandra. *Decentralization and the City Schools: Looking Forward,* No. 12 in a Series of Occasional Papers. New York: League for Industrial Democracy, 1968. In ERIC Abstracts *Citizen Involvement in the Control of Schools.* Eugene: University of Oregon, 1970.

Freedom, Bureaucracy, and Schooling. Washington D. C.: Association for Supervision and Curriculum Development, 1971.

Lee, Gordon C., ed. *Crusade Against Ignorance: Thomas Jefferson on Education.* New York: Bureau of Publications, Teachers College, 1961.

Lopate, Carol, et al. *Some Effects of Parent and Community Participation in Public Education,* ERIC-IRDC Urban Disadvantaged Series, No. 3, February 1969. In ERIC Abstracts *Citizen Involvement in the Control of Schools.* Eugene: University of Oregon, 1970.

Miller, Van. *The Public Administration of American School Systems.* New York: Macmillan, 1965.

Peterson, Paul E. "The Politics of American Education." *Review of Research in Education.* Ed. Fred N. Kerlinger and John B. Carroll. Itasca, Ill.: F. E. Peacock, 1974. II, 348–90.

"What America Thinks of Itself," *Newsweek,* 10 December 1973, pp. 40, 45–46.

The Schools and the Economic System

	Individual in Focus	Group in Focus
Task	→ Economic System ← ALLOCATION →Vocational Education←	
Membership		

ECONOMICS AS ALLOCATION

Once a group has defined its goals, members must be assigned roles that will accomplish various tasks to bring about the shared and common purpose. Suppose the school board decides a new school is needed. To raise money to cover construction costs, bonds must be sold by the district director of finance. Blueprints must be drawn and reviewed, and construction overseen, possibly by a school plant manager. The director of personnel selects more teachers. Regardless of whether a school district has specialized ascribed roles like these directors, the superintendent must assign all these tasks and many more if children are to attend that school as planned.

Assigning roles, like defining goals, focuses upon the task dimension of group life—for example, raising money, determining the pitch of the roof, hiring personnel. Both these group functions are concerned with the work or task of the group rather than with the membership functions of integration and socialization.

In the transformational model placing role assignment under the column headed "Individual in Focus" is somewhat arbitrary. Surely, individuals do hold roles, and individuals fill roles in highly individualistic ways, no matter what society's expectations. Also, identifiably different tasks are required to accomplish a common purpose. But despite differences in tasks, there is interdependence. Directors of personnel, finance, and plant management do different jobs, but if the work of each is to pay off in the school, each has to rely on the work of the others as well. Thus role assignment implies complementarity between assigned roles (as in the separate duties of a team of teachers) as well as specialization of task to accomplish a group's purpose. Educational departmentalization at the secondary-school level is also an illustration of this concept. If the goal is to get the students in the tenth grade properly educated for their level of attainment, the tasks assigned English teachers, science teachers, and shop teachers are particular and specific—though all the teachers share the same educational purpose, namely, socialization of this group of teenagers.

The body of human knowledge called *economics* is concerned with the processes by which a society allocates resources that are scarce to meet a demand that is considered to be unlimited. Generally, economists concentrate on the production and distribution of oil, food, and other materials—or, to use the economists' term "goods." How are these limited goods assigned to the many people who are in need of them? A pure capitalist system responds, "In proportion to their ability freely to purchase them." An ideal communist system claims, "According to their need for them." In real life neither economic philosophy operates in its pure form, but differences in these significant values cause differences in the economic choices of communist and noncommunist nations.

Besides scarce material goods, services that workers provide are also allocated among competing needs. American schools in slums or remote farming communities may find it difficult to obtain a supply of teachers to meet their demands for educational service. Most teachers are unwilling to sell their services in these areas. In the Soviet Union teachers are allocated arbitrarily by the government to such posts, since social need determines who teaches where.

In industrialized civilizations, in order to supply many competing needs, money to purchase goods and services itself may be in demand. Schools are allocated money by society out of the taxes collected. But other social needs, such as highways and welfare, are also in competition for those scarce tax dollars.

How much of society's available resources of money, goods, and services ought to be spent on education? Most businesses can identify how much it will cost to implement various production methods in order to deliver a specific product. But a precise answer to this cost effectiveness question in education is impossible without strictly limiting the goals of education. Further, it is presently almost impossible to identify in exact quantitative terms what effect will result from spending money on a variable like "classroom atmosphere" or how worthwhile the outcome of "interpreting information" is. Efforts are being made by persons both within and without schools to move toward the business model of product cost, but it will not be an easy task. While specific judgments cannot be made at this time, there is evidence that a nation does profit economically as the proportion of national resources allocated to education rises. (M. Carnoy, 1967) The more money supplied to schools, the more the return to society. Further, as countries acquire increasingly technological economies, the value of schooling increases proportionally. A major reason is the schools' elevation of unskilled or semiskilled workers by training in industrially valuable skills.

The economics of the educational system focuses upon these two particular processes of allocation—the delegation of tax monies to provide the service of education, and the expectation by society that in return the schools shall provide people who can be allocated as workers and consumers within the economic system. We will discuss each of these two processes in turn, with special emphasis toward the end of the chapter on the failure of the contemporary school system to meet its vocational and consumer-education roles.

THE SCHOOLS AS CONSUMERS OF ALLOCATED GOODS AND SERVICES

What Do Schools Consume?

The place of education in our economy is an important one. According to one authority:

> The schooling industry now represents between 6% and 7% of the total [American economy]. . . . It is now a larger segment . . . than agriculture and there are good reasons for supposing that it will continue to grow at least until the end of the century. (Kenneth Boulding, 1972, p. 129)

More Americans earn their living by providing the service of schoolteaching than by doing any other single job. We provide about one teacher for every twenty children between six and sixteen plus other adults for those older and younger. That makes up a large slice of the salary pie in our country.

Further, schools occupy land and buildings. They buy books and light bulbs. They use up scarce resources that the economy cannot allocate to some other use. Money for school construction decreases the amount available for state hospitals.

With the school-leaving age raised higher and higher, the labor resources of young people are "consumed" by the schools, which hold youths in classrooms rather than letting them enter the fields and factories to produce goods and services for the rest of the economy. The population trend that diminishes the number of young people in our society is balanced by a tendency for each to wish more education. The longer a student remains in school, the greater the cost to the economy in the loss of his or her work time.

How Are the Schools Financed?

Private schools and colleges are supported in greatest part by tuition fees and grants from religious and secular foundations. The vast majority of the colleges and schools of the United States, however, are supported by money acquired by taxing citizens.

Nineteenth-century financial support for public schools was drawn from where the wealth lay in a preindustrial agricultural community, namely, the land. Local taxes on property still are the major financial resource supporting public schools. There is, however, increasing pressure to change to some other form of tax support. This is due to two forms of inequity that property taxes create.

Most Americans support the concept of equalization of the tax burden across all levels of income. The graduated federal income tax is an example of this value in action. Those who have more, pay more, although they are left with a significantly greater residue than the poor. Taxes that fall with a harder burden on the poor, taking a greater proportion of their money, are called *regressive taxes*. A general sales tax is the best example of this: the poor spend proportionately more of their income on necessities like food and clothing than do the rich. Taxes on these items, therefore, take more from the poor than the rich.

The property taxes that support schools are also regressive upon the poor. Landowners pass on the property tax to their tenants hidden in the rent (although the government sometimes provides a rent subsidy to the poor to relieve this tax burden). If the poor own a home, the tax upon it represents a bigger proportion of their income than the tax on the homes of the rich. Many Americans feel such inequality is essentially undemocratic.

Historically, local districts have been empowered by the state to levy and raise taxes on property. This local revenue is usually the major source of tax funds for schools. States, however, also supplement local revenues with funds that are raised by statewide taxes on private or corporation income, or sales taxes of one form or another. Of course, John Q. Public "donates" the money for all these taxes, whether it goes directly to his local school board via a tax on his home or gets there by way of the state's tax upon his income or the customs duty on his foreign purchases.

There is a second form of inequity in the property tax. It arises because there is a difference in wealth between school districts due to variations in the *tax base*, or value of property that is available for taxing. One must also consider the number of children who must share the educational services supported by the tax base.

One district in the Middle Atlantic states has a major interstate bridge and its approaches, an interstate highway, the state hospital for the mentally ill, and a large cemetery within its small boundaries. All of these property uses are tax exempt (a way a modern society helps other group needs than education). This property contributes nothing to the education of district children. At the same time, this particular district has few factories or office buildings. These properties are desirable to have because they pay high taxes but contribute few children to the school rolls. The land from which money can be raised, the tax base of this district, is therefore minimal.

A nearby district in the same state has few tax-free lands except several cemeteries. It does, however, have a huge industrial complex that provides millions of dollars in taxes for the few thousand children that live within the school district.

If you divide the property wealth in each district by the number of children in each district, you will find that these neighboring school districts in the same state have vastly different amounts to spend on their pupils.

In addition to such differences between districts as these, there are also vast differences in the tax base of urban and rural areas. Since World War II much industry has fled the city, and the property values of homes have generally fallen. Tax-exempt properties like hospitals, museums, and libraries are clustered in cities. Metropolitan areas have seen rising costs in all the services they must offer, with tax funds to meet those costs diminishing. City schools must scramble to obtain from urban governments sufficient operational funds; the competition is great.

In rural areas, industry may be undeveloped, with property tax money coming in greatest part from farms. But farms are assessed at low value in order to support the vital agricultural sector of our economy.

The result of these factors has brought about a form of taxation so inequitably raised and distributed that former United States Commissioner of Education Harold Howe II has branded it all but obsolete. (Howe, 1971)

Equalization. Inequities such as these have been partially compensated for by a process known as *equalization.* The state supplements local districts with funds in inverse proportion to the district's ability to raise taxes on property. Thus citizens of richer districts pay for the education of the tax-poor districts by redistribution of income and sales taxes paid to the state.

A 1972 court case in California *(Serrano* v. *Priest)* decided that any difference in the funds available for each student resident of the state was in violation of the civil rights of the individual students as described in the California constitution. The Supreme Court of the United States agreed that differences were in violation of the California bill of rights and ordered the state to further equalize the amount of tax money available to each California student. However, at the same session, in a case coming from Texas (which did not have a state bill of rights) the Supreme Court decided that such differences were not in violation of civil rights as spelled out in the federal Constitution. Texas, therefore, did not have to equalize tax support among Texas pupils.

Obviously, this issue needs to be further clarified. An interesting question arises on what will be the next step if further *intrastate* differences are declared unconstitutional. Will *interstate* differences be allowed to stand? Mississippi students each year have thousands of dollars less spent on them than do their fellow pupils in New York and California. Do you believe that is consistent with the ideal of equal rights Americans hold? Would you be willing to sacrifice the local control of schools in order to equalize the educational opportunity between students in various districts and states of our country?

Inequitable distribution of funds within individual districts has often been offered as evidence of unequal segregated education. Cases requiring desegregation of schools in the cities of Detroit and Boston during the 1970s resulted from these discrepancies. Since a larger segment of black families than white are poor, these parents were contributing proportionately more in taxes while their children were getting less back in school!

Tax Levying by Way of Referendum. State governments also permit local districts to raise additional tax money by special "referenda." Generally, these requests for funds are proposed by local school boards, and citizens of the district vote (usually in a special election) whether or not to tax themselves further to support their schools. Referenda may raise the percentage of the property tax, add new revenue sources, or permit the issuance of bonds backed by the credit of the district. When taxpayers are disgusted with the operation of their schools or, unfortunately, when they are disgusted with other levels of government that tax without asking permission so directly, they frequently vote against referenda. No matter how badly schools need more money—double sessions, overcrowded classrooms, or out-of-date textbooks notwithstanding—if a referendum doesn't pass, there is no additional local money to spend. No wonder schools conduct intensive publicity campaigns to get out the vote. Still, few laymen and few teachers bother to vote. Usually only the disgruntled come out in force.

Tax Levying at the State Level. The state legislature is asked to vote the taxes that provide the state supplements for education. If the legislators decide that the educators are not doing the job their constituents demand, or if they think they can court the favor of voters by reducing or cutting taxes, once again the schools may go begging for funds. Contracts with teachers may be held up until the start of a new term while a legislative body decides how much of the state's budget will be allocated to meet the schools' demand. A new highway or an environmental protection agency may seem more urgent to the legislators if vested interests or the public are pressuring them.

Because salaries and working conditions of school personnel are so much at the whim of legislators whose decisions are based on balancing more forces than schools alone, teachers in the last twenty years have banded together to exert pressure directly upon them. This is discussed under the section "Are Schools a Business?" below.

Other Revenue Sources Besides Taxes. Local and state school districts are also allowed to raise funds by selling bonds, which are repaid with interest out of the tax funds expected to be collected by the district in future years. This method is often used for raising funds needed quickly for an expanding building program. There are limitations upon the amount of money that a district can raise so that it will not go over its debt ceiling—the amount of money it can legally borrow. Such limitations may hobble a school if its rapidly expanding school population needs a roof over its head on days of required school attendance. On the other hand, even with a debt ceiling, a district can overextend itself and be saddled for years with expenses of interest and principal on bonds—expenses that use up a significant portion of funds that might otherwise be allocated to the other needs of the schools.

Districts that had to rush school construction to meet burgeoning entering school populations in the 1960s found themselves with empty elementary classrooms—even whole buildings—in the 1970s when the birth rate fell rapidly. While the population bulge of the last decade continues to burden junior and senior high schools, superintendents are considering ways of utilizing the empty buildings, whose bond interest still constitutes a healthy portion of each year's annual school budget.

Are Schools a Business?

How Schools Are Like Business. There are many indications that schools act like a big business. It is not unusual, for instance, to have school-district administrators make as much as governors or local managers and be in charge of as many employees and as vast an industrial plant. Moreover, the management of most schools parallels the management of industries. This is because both use the bureaucratic form of control. As we pointed out in the last chapter, the bureaucratic form of management has some negative educational characteristics. But much that attracted businesspeople to bureaucratic forms is also attractive to school administrators. There is, for example, an emphasis upon rationality in decision-making processes. Personal whim is reduced to a minimum. Reasons for decisions can and are made known to all. Conflicts may be resolved objectively and impersonally. The American value of "efficiency" makes bureaucracy worthwhile to schools. As David Goslin has noted, "More efficient uses have been made of teacher time and effort by such practices as team teaching, the use of master teachers, television lectures, and the introduction of specialists in areas like reading and foreign language instruction." (Goslin, 1965, p. 47)

On the other hand, because bureaucracy favors permanence (by establishing the way to carry out a task), hierarchical decision making, and a division of labor, it also tends to perpetuate the status quo. Thus, present-day critics of the school suggest that bureaucratic structure did not arise either to match the society in which the schools live or to produce efficiency, but rather to perpetuate the power of the wealthy over the poor and the white upper class over minority subcultures.

In support of this conclusion, Michael Katz states that power-holding elements in New England society specifically set up schools bureaucratically so that they might keep control over the educational opportunities offered immigrants flooding into the country. By this method those who held a vested interest in the status quo were able to maintain it against the pressure of the new members of their already established society. (Katz, 1971) Another pair of researchers, William Cave and Mark Chesler, draw a somewhat similar picture. They substitute the dominance of whites over all other ethnic cultures in our country as the rationale for many present school practices. (Cave and Chesler, 1974)

Whatever the motivation for the installation of bureaucracy, in the last hundred years school systems have become giant corporations whose boards of directors (school boards) have little knowledge or control over their managers (superintendents and other educational administrators). This follows the trend in American businesses, where ownership and management have also become separate. Thus, stockholders in IBM or ITT today have little direction over the companies they own. It is not surprising then that over the years teachers have moved to counterbalance the thrust of the managers and decision makers of education, just as the American labor movement organized to have some force in the decisions of American industry.

This political organization of teachers was slow in coming.

The National Education Association (NEA) was formed in 1857, and for the first hundred years it emphasized that it was "a professional organization." Many teachers, coming from lower-class or lower-middle-class backgrounds, took pride in seeing themselves as professionals like doctors and lawyers. They avoided bargaining and strikes because they associated these with the action of unions of persons beneath them in class and scholastic preparation. Further, as public servants, many teachers felt that it was improper, if not illegal, to strike against the public interest. Many said they "owed it to the children" to stay on the job.

In 1916 another, more feisty organization—the American Federation of Teachers (AFT)—began. It sought support from and identification with organized labor and is now an affiliate of the American Federation of Labor—Congress of Industrial Organizations (AFL-CIO). Since 1955 the AFT has become representative of more and more teachers, especially those in urban areas. Not at all ashamed to strike or boycott, the AFT has brought rewards to teacher members similar to those earned by other unions. The force of this growing younger brother has caused the NEA to adapt a more militant approach to teachers' welfare and rights. It is not unusual now for a local NEA to strike or threaten to strike in order to force its demands upon those who are making decisions about salary and working conditions. And a new member has joined the administrative team of many school districts—the full-time labor negotiator.

While both AFT and NEA officials usually emphasize that the welfare of school-children is their primary concern, they appear to see that welfare best served by the same kinds of wage increases, hour reductions, and lessened workloads that any other labor organization advocates for its members. Educators as employees are no more unique than administrators as employers in the education business. Both managers and workers in schools play roles strikingly like those in private enterprise.

How Schools Differ from Business. As many similarities as there are between school and business, the school system is far from a private, free competitive enterprise. Economist Kenneth Boulding has described how difficult it is to trace what connection, if any, exists between the product of schools and the goods and services which are allocated to them. For this reason, education simply cannot operate as do other industries. (Boulding, 1972) As we alluded to earlier in this chapter, although schools are expected to produce knowledge in various forms, none of these forms is easy to measure. How much better are 400 B.A.s than 450 (or 350) B.Ed.s? It costs more to produce B.A.s than B.Ed.s, but are they worth more? If so, is it economically efficient to spend more money upon them because of the greater return on our money? What inputs make a better product? What thermometer measures the emotional warmth of a classroom? What electroencephalogram charts "intellectual curiosity"? What facts are available for rational decision making by school managers?

Money comes to education in the form of grants. The size and allocation of these grants are determined by many pressures, such as the size of a tax base or the militancy of a teachers' union. These financial allocations have almost nothing to do with the quality or quantity of the product, even assuming that one could properly measure units of knowledge. In order to make schools more accountable for these monies, attempts are being made to quantify educational objectives and inputs. But as we have noted and will discuss in detail in Chapter 8, such quantification is difficult.

Further, the public schools as the educational institution established by the government represent a state *monopoly* that supports private competitive business by supplying a skilled labor force. This sort of mixed economy is not unusual in modern capitalism. Most businesses and labor organizations look to the central government to continue the long line of special services that keep them "in business." Oil depletion allowances and closed shop legislation are two examples of this in the general economy. However, lack of significant competition within the established educational system prevents a truly free market in schooling. Few can choose where to buy their education. This results in the same kind of problems that economic monopoly brings about in other segments of the economy.

When a single business controls an industry, the public is infrequently offered prime quality or a choice among products. The supply and price of the product are solely in the hands of the single producer. What can you do to take your business elsewhere for telephone service? In school you may take only the scope and sequence of material that is offered. In a free market the consumer's choice provides thumbs-up on good products and services, thumbs-down on inefficient operations. Poor businesses are soon driven out of business. But with required attendance laws, no public school will be closed down due to a lack of customers for its product.

As with other monopolistic businesses, lack of competition can cause inefficiency and extravagant waste of money, time, and personnel. Today many critics are dissatisfied with the methods and results of the American school system. They believe the way to improve the quality of education is to break this monopoly. They propose to disestablish, or withdraw official state recognition, from schools. National churches were disestablished in the eighteenth century and no longer received support, financial or otherwise, from governments. Perhaps the government should get out of the education business as well and let a free school market provide a variety of educational opportunities.

Establishing Competition: The Voucher System. As desirable as a free market in education may be, establishing it would be a difficult task. The poor have too little money to spend on food and shelter, much less provide their children with private education. Thus, complete independence and an absolutely open buyers' market would not guarantee meeting the needs of the whole society for intelligent voters and employable workers—the two major aims of the school system.

An alternative to established or privately funded schools is the *voucher system.* In this case, the state gives each child a voucher, or cash receipt, representing his quota of tax money. With this, the child (or the child's parents) may purchase an education at the school of his or her choice. The expectation is that schools that better meet the needs of students and parents will prosper, and those that are inefficient and wasteful will "wither away," just as inefficient and wasteful businesses are supposed to do in an economy with free choice.

Despite these arguments for the voucher system, there are numerous arguments against this proposal as well. Some persons are concerned that very homogeneous, self-segregated schools would develop. Moreover, vocational schools with high overhead costs (due to their need for special equipment) might find it hard to make ends meet. And parents might select schools that did not adequately meet the needs of society as a whole. Lastly, if restrictions were put on voucher-supported schools to insure that racial, religious, or economic discrimination was not practiced, ultimate control might return to a governmental agency, the very situation a voucher system is supposed to remedy.

The arguments against have not deterred interest in this alternative. In the mid-1970s the United States government supported a pilot program of the voucher system in the San Jose (California) school district. This allowed pupils and their parents to choose among schools of that district. A menu of offerings included a "back to basics" curriculum, stressing a traditional education, and an open school, permitting wider student options. (These alternatives are discussed in greater detail in Chapters 6 and 7.) Other school districts, however, have been slow to adopt this form of education support.

Can you think of any other arguments pro and con on this new idea to transform schools?

SCHOOLS AS PRODUCERS

The History of the Vocational Role of Schools

As we noted at the beginning, in return for allocating resources to schools, society has always expected that schools would prepare young members for places in the economic structure. An ongoing society needs a continuous supply of newly trained workers.

However, since the days of ancient Greece, this societal expectation has been in conflict with another goal of education—to impart knowledge for knowledge's sake. The concern for balancing a *liberal arts education* (stressing general studies to produce a cultured person) and *vocational education* (whose outcome is a productive worker) was evident in the writing of many American educators, including Thomas Jefferson, Horace Mann, and John Dewey. (Lawrence Cremin, 1965)

Among the Athenian Greeks the issue was settled by including in the core of seven liberal arts subjects some vocationally useful subjects—astronomy for guiding a sea merchant's ships, rhetoric to aid a young Greek in forcefully presenting his ideas in assembly, and music to refresh his spirit after fulfilling all his civic duties. This broader curriculum was called "liberal" (from the Latin for freedom) because a wiser man was considered a freer man since he would be able to choose from a wider variety of alternatives.

When after the Dark Ages of Europe, the founders of the medieval universities looked back on the shining light of classical Greece and Rome, they adopted the liberal arts curriculum as the base upon which a gentleman might build his professional training in medicine, law, and the church. Early Latin schools equipped adolescent males with a knowledge of that language so that they might study the classical tradition and thereby gain a foundation for their chosen occupation. The survival of Latin in today's schools is a frequently noted example of educational entropy.

This balance in education of liberal arts and vocational concerns was disturbed by the Industrial Revolution. Trevor Burridge, an educational historian, believes that in the wake of the tremendous expansion of goods and services following the Industrial Revolution:

> [there] has been a veritable obsession with the idea of education as the key to material success both for the individual and for society. Of all the original aims of mass education, it is the vocational one that has come down to us in its purest form and has indeed been reinforced in recent years. (Burridge, 1970, p. 119)

Before the Industrial Revolution society needed a fairly small number of professionals who required advanced training. Skilled workers could learn their vocations by being apprenticed to masters of the art they would follow. And agricultural workers and others who needed only minimum skills learned "on the job." The Industrial Revolution meant that machines had to be tended with varying degrees of care. Society needed many workers with a wide variety of skills.

For the universities this meant expanding the professional training they offered. Little by little, new vocations were accepted as equally worthy as the ancient professions of medicine, law, and theology. Graduate studies in science, engineering, and education were admitted in the eighteenth and nineteenth centuries. Those most liberal of the arts—music and fine arts—also came to be recognized as worthy of vocational training in the university. In the final stages, as a college degree became a prerequisite for entrance into middle-management positions in business, colleges were given the job of preparing the increasing number of bureaucrats and managers for the economic system.

This vocational emphasis in college education has probably affected you personally as well. Ask yourself and your friends (and not just those in the "trade school" of educational classes) why you are in college. The answer will probably come back, "Because I want to be a ——— (fill in the profession)." Rarely does a liberal arts student reply, "Because I want to learn to be more wise."

While colleges and universities have included more and more vocational education in their curricula, high schools have followed the same trend. Originally conceived almost exclusively as preparatory schools for higher education, the high schools have assumed a greater and greater responsibility for training youth for employment immediately upon graduation.

This trend started in the middle of the nineteenth century, when millions of immigrants came flooding into this country. These newcomers needed to be integrated into the expanding and diversifying American economic system. Schools were expected to prepare the population for jobs at all levels of skill. As the demand increased for higher and higher levels of competence, technical education was expanded within and above high schools. In our century technical institutes and two-year colleges have opened.

Changes in our economic system have therefore put tremendous pressures on the educational system to fill a wide variety of worker roles. Much of this pressure falls on the public-school system, the job of which is now to train and (by implication) to help allocate workers to various slots from top to bottom in our economic system.

How Do the Schools Help Allocate Workers?

The school system sorts out who should fill what economic role in the same way one selects various grades of peas for packaging. Those who "fall out" first along the educational line take the unskilled jobs so long as they are available; after that they are unemployed. Completion of several years of high school sends drop-outs to semiskilled positions. High-school or vocational school graduation may guarantee a white-collar or skilled vocation, while college (two years of technical training or a bachelor's degree) opens the door to the professional or paraprofessional vocations. The high moneymakers in our economy—doctors, lawyers, accountants—are made up of those who survive several years of graduate school as well. The exceptions to this school allocation process—the drop-out millionaire and the "ski bum" Princeton graduate—stand out because they *are* unique.

Clearly, success in contemporary American society is related to success in the American school system. The screening process of publicly financed schools provides the private entrepreneur with "low-cost information on probable differences in worker productivity which can be used for screening prospective employees." (Finis Welch, 1974, p. 195) There is, however, much doubt whether success in school *causes* success in one's vocation.

A major part of the continuing American dream has been that because schooling is universal and comprehensive, open to all, each person has the opportunity to succeed. As recently as 1968, one of the most respected journals in education, *Phi Delta Kappan*, published an article that articulated the supposed role of education in the American dream:

> American education has not been stratified in the European sense, and largely because of the fact it has produced outstanding achievement: social mobility. Social mobility contributes not only to a healthy and growing economy but to the maintenance of a free political system. Sons of immigrant fruit peddlers become owners of restaurants or doctors; sons of poor farmers become university presidents or bankers; and the sons of police officers and plumbers are elected mayors or members of

Congress. Without a system of comprehensive and high quality
education, social mobility would be a far less significant factor
in our economic and political life. (Ira Polley, 1968, p. 13)

Each of us can point to individuals whose lives seem to exem-
plify this view of American education. To believe that it has
characterized the great majority of Americans, however, is to
believe in a legend not based on fact. Success in school *and*
success in a career are both influenced by a third factor—
characteristics of one's parents.

In 1966 James Coleman published *Equal Educational Opportunity*, the results of his study regarding the impact of racial
integration upon previously legally desegregated schools. He
found that the most important determiner of school achievement was the income level of the majority of the parents in a
school. While many reevaluations of the massive statistics of
Coleman's study and similar investigations have been made,
this single result dominates all generalizations about school
success: achievement of pupils is primarily related to the income level of the majority of parents in the school.

Racial composition of the student body, ratio of the number
of teachers to the number of pupils, size of the school library,
and other "school effects" like these appear to have no impact
on achievement except as they are indirect measures of the
income of parents in a school district. (F. Mosteller and D. P.
Moynihan, 1972) How parental income actually influences pupil performance is not yet clear. Most researchers assume that
the parents' level of expectation is conveyed by pupils into the
classroom, and this establishes the norm of academic conduct
and achievement that influences the group as a whole and individuals within the group.

Other recent research confirms the validity of Coleman's original study. Christopher Jencks pursued the Coleman data with
even more refined statistical analysis. He concluded that
schools had no measurable impact at all upon pupil vocational
achievement in adult life and that the single strongest influence was the income level of the individual's father. (Jencks,
1972) Colin Greer studied drop-out rates of immigrant groups
to this country in the nineteenth and early twentieth centuries.
His research showed that "the school's ability to retain pupils

coincides with and seems to be dominated by that group's simultaneously recorded adult employment rate ... cultural background and economic status being reflected and reinforced in the school, not caused by it." (Greer, 1972, pp. 83 and 85)

So, it now appears that, in a general sense, success in the American school is determined by the success of one's parents in the American economy, which also determines the individual's own out-of-school success.

Many factors related to the income of pupils' parents tend to compound, that is, they act to change each other rather than simply adding their various influences. This interaction makes it very difficult to identify for groups of students (never mind for an individual student) exactly what is the impact of each piece of the education-economics mix. Parental attitudes toward the promise of education, the number of like-class parents in the school population, the match of parent-pupil values with middle-class teachers, the amount of taxes parents are willing to take on to support schools—all relate to parental socioeconomic status. (Figure 5.1 in Chapter 5 shows how family factors also interact within the student himself.)

Staying in school is a result of all these factors, but is school success just a shadow of the reality of a pupil's social class, or does something "rub off" in all those years in schools that makes pupils more or less valuable as employees?

Of course, if a student has learned how to wire a house while in school, he or she has a specific skill that is usually vocationally valuable. Given a need for electricians, the student has a passport to a role in our economic system because of specific occupational preparation. But most employers seek high-school or college graduates simply because they have completed a certain number of sessions in the educational system, not caring what curriculum was pursued.

The learning that "pays off" apparently is not so much skills like readin' and 'rithmetic, but rather attitudes and habits of behavior. Educators are no longer quite so bold as G. Stanley Hall, who advocated in 1892 that "for most of us, the best education is that which makes us the best and most obedient servants." (Hall, p. 86)

What attitudes and habits, then, did the Industrial Revolution demand in order to work in an assembly-line, free-enterprise, bureaucratic economy? The very habits and attitudes that educational historians identify as the dominant lessons of American schools: "Toleration of boredom, learning as memorization, competition and hostility." (Greer, 1972, p. 152) "Punctuality counted, as did loyalty and obedience." (Henry Perkinson, 1968, p. 111)

Looking at your own schooling, you may be able to recall innumerable instances of such lessons. You probably practiced them this week in your college classrooms.

New Knowledge from Research and Development

In today's highly industrialized society, the highest levels of education fulfill a third function in addition to vocational and liberal arts training. Utilizing the scholar's curiosity and the university's laboratories, both government and business now look to the universities to supply the major portion of activity in research and development. This task is accomplished by granting to colleges, departments, or individual professors money to be spent on enlarging the fields of knowledge that government or business feel are worthwhile. As with the National Defense Education Act, such available money frequently is the crucial factor in selecting programs and emphases on campus, in deciding which professors remain and which unsuccessful grant proposal writers are let go. Contracts for these research activities now comprise a major portion of the budgets of many universities.

Not surprisingly, with pressures toward such a variety of goals, the 1970 Carnegie Commission on Higher Education listed as the first priority of colleges a clear definition of the purpose or purposes of the institutions, after which all other priorities might be ordered more rationally.

EDUCATIONAL ENTROPY: VOCATIONAL EDUCATION

The first Industrial Revolution of the seventeenth and eighteenth centuries was set off by the application of water and steam power to machinery. Throughout the second Industrial

Revolution of the nineteenth century, machinery took over more and more jobs that had previously been accomplished by brute strength or manual skill of humans. In the early decades of the twentieth century, the industrial organization that we can loosely identify as the assembly line demanded great numbers of semiskilled workers—persons less trained than skilled craftspeople but more trained than workers with no salable trade.

As this century draws to a close, however, we find ourselves in the middle of a third Industrial Revolution. Nowadays the brute strength of unskilled workers seldom brings a job; further, machines have taken over almost all the semiskilled jobs that were the backbone of employment in the days of Henry Ford; and finally, machines are beginning to do the work of human brains. Computerization permits machines to make simple decisions and the "human use of human beings" becomes daily more restricted to those with highly technical skills or those who can make decisions too complex or value-laden for computers to decide.

Given these new economic realities, how beneficial is vocational education in the United States today? "Disastrous" answers a headline describing the January 1975 report of the federal General Accounting Office.

> Government programs for vocational education—training designed to prepare students in public high schools and two year colleges for jobs—are generally pictured as disasters in a new report to Congress by the General Accounting Office.
>
> The watchdog agency found that students are often trained for jobs that do not exist and that only about a third of the students in vocational education courses wind up employed in the skill they learned in school. (*The Morning News*, Wilmington, Delaware, 8 January 1975, p. 5)

Because of the rapidly changing nature of modern technology, the entry-level skill that school graduates may bring (if they are among the happy third mentioned above) will not assist them as they are forced to make one job change after another throughout their working lives. The major portion of specific occupational skill training will come on these jobs, long after the workers leave school.

Still, Welch found in studying Latin American countries that the more advanced the agricultural or protoindustrial base of the economy in a developing country, the greater the return on the country's investment in education. The clue to this apparent paradox comes in the school-taught skills that were the most beneficial: (1) decoding data (a somewhat fancy term for "reading" and its spin-off abilities such as deciphering a computer's print-out), and (2) an ability to evaluate information. Apparently, the attitudes and habits of behavior needed by tomorrow's work force are almost antithetical to those the traditional school has inculcated. Learning must shift from memorization to facile ingenuity, obedience to responsible decision making, and competition to the teamwork needed for consideration of all factors in a highly technological environment.

Some of the basic skills schools must now teach in order to fulfill their reciprocal role with the economic system include the ability to transfer knowledge, to generalize concepts, to evaluate decisions, and to adjust rapidly to new work situations and new groups of fellow workers. These skills can be loosely grouped under the title of "learning how to learn"—an ability (and a motivation) to continue to educate oneself and to be educated long after leaving the schoolroom. The school cannot transmit the culture of tomorrow; we shall have to learn it as we live it. But the school can teach ways to learn and evaluate a culture, no matter how it changes before our eyes.

How will your teaching foster these new attitudes and behaviors? It's not impossible to begin to structure schooling to meet the needs of the new generations of workers. But this is only part of the impact of the "knowledge explosion." What responsibility should the schools have for educating the increasingly large number of boys and girls who will simply not be needed for the constantly decreasing number of jobs that only humans can accomplish? What schooling is useful for the "vocationally superfluous"? What will school mean to a majority of youth when it obviously no longer provides the entrance to job placement? Motivation to learn can no longer depend on eventual vocational relevance. What transformation does this suggest?

THE CONSUMER SOCIETY

The majority of citizens in a postindustrial society will have no place to be employed, even if they are intellectually capable of mastering the skills exhibited by one of the few employed persons. They may be occupationally useless.

They will not, however, be economically superfluous. As consumers, their demand is needed to keep money flowing between production and distribution. As long as the American public continues to demand color TVs and individual pleasure cars (one per family member as a minimum ideal), the great production lines of the United States will continue to roll. Classical economics supposes that the demand for such goods and services is by nature unlimited. In practice, advertising functions to create and sustain a demand that, when realized in the marketplace, sustains high levels of production and employment in the American economy.

Massive unemployability, like massive unemployment, eliminates wages to purchase goods, which dooms the flow of the economy. When depression looms, government rushes to increase citizens' purchasing power to refuel flickering production. The dissolution of demand because of a decrease in the work force could be overcome by allocating purchase money to all, regardless of their ability to be placed in the work system. This is the rationale for providing Americans with a guaranteed annual wage—a minimum allowance with which all could consume, regardless of their ability or opportunity to produce.

It may be that in the future schools will have to take on a different role than they have played before in educating consumers. Heretofore, the schools have used consumer education classes to refine rather than manipulate consumer demand; that is, they have sought to improve buying decisions rather than to plant a desire for consumption itself. Now the rest of society may expect its schools to educate youth to demand the rich high standard of living that the Industrial Revolution fostered as a part of the value that "more equals better." The commercial mass media, however, are currently doing a splendid job of urging demand to higher and higher levels. They need little help from schools.

On the other hand, if the schools were to foster a simpler, less materially oriented society such as suggested in revolutionary volumes like Theodore Roszak's *The Making of the Counter-Culture* (1969), the American economy would be faced with a massive adjustment. Unemployment in the industries producing products no longer in demand would rise. Imagine what would happen in Detroit if more bikes than cars are purchased.

MAIN IDEAS

1. Economics is the social process that assigns the scarce resources of goods and services to meet unlimited needs (demands).
2. While a group purpose is shared in common by all members, assigned roles to accomplish the purpose are filled by individuals, frequently in individualistic ways.
3. Money to purchase the economic goods and services schools demand is allocated from limited tax funds.
4. Property taxes, which have been the major support of schools, are now seen as an out-of-date method of taxation.
5. States provide supplemental funds to equalize tax funds available to local districts.
6. Voting on school referenda gives the public a chance to express approval or disapproval of their schools.
7. Schools are like big business in size, structure, and control by competing forces.
8. Teachers' organizations parallel other worker unions in a concern for "bread and butter" issues.
9. Schools differ from business because they do not operate in a free-enterprise marketplace. There is little connection between the product of schools and the money granted to them. And the "price" for educating the young does not readily reflect changes in either supply or demand.
10. The established public schools are a no-competition monopoly. Critics suggest this is one reason they do not meet the needs of their consumers, that is, students.

11. An alternative to a monopolistic or totally free educational system is a public voucher plan.
12. Vocational education is an extensive and historical reciprocal responsibility of schools to the economic system.
13. Schools allocate workers to the various levels of skill and training that modern technical society demands by a sorting process.
14. The sorting takes place as a result of parents' income, which affects not only a number of school resources, but more significantly the norm of expected pupil achievement.
15. Schools provide two types of vocationally valuable training: (a) specific occupational skills and (b) work-worthy attitudes and behaviors.
16. The work behaviors and attitudes that were valuable to the economy at the dawn of the twentieth century are no longer so in the postindustrial society. Schools may be able to meet modern needs by training pupils to "learn how to learn" new kinds of basic skills and attitudes.
17. Since an increasing proportion of the population will be unemployable in the future, schools must seek new methods of motivation and retention.
18. Expanded consumer education is a possible avenue for continued economic service by the school system. Such education may either perpetuate or radically alter accepted economic values.

GLOSSARY

economics   The processes by which resources are allocated to meet varied needs.

equalization   Money provided by states to overcome inequities between local districts in available tax monies.

liberal arts education   The general studies that since the Renaissance have been seen as necessary for the proper education of a cultured person.

monopoly   Control of one segment of the economy by a single business, as opposed to competition among many suppliers in an open market.

referendum   A question on a ballot asking the public to decide an issue. In the case of schools, it is usually a proposed tax.

regressive taxes   Taxes that fall with inequitable weight on poorer persons.

tax base   The wealth that can support our social needs. In the case of schools, it is usually synonomous with the value of property in the local district.

vocational education   Education whose function is to train workers for a job.

vcucher system   A plan that would in effect return tax money to students in the form of a receipt that they could cash in at the school of their choice in payment for their education.

SUGGESTED ACTIVITIES

1. Discover what percentage of your state budget is allocated to education. How does this compare with other states? What factors determine the costs shared by local districts? Does your state have an equalization formula?

2. Attend the Joint Finance Committee meetings of your state legislature. Analyze the observable interactions as suggested in the activities section for Chapter 2.

3. Check newspaper files on schools that are attempting various "accountability" programs. You might also investigate "merit pay." Interviews with teachers, administrators, and students might be profitable.

4. Do institutions of higher learning within your state differ in their emphasis upon career as opposed to liberal arts curricula? Can you identify present and/or historical reasons for these differences in emphasis?

5. How many vocationally oriented and how many liberal arts courses are required for teacher certification in your state?

What changes have been made in the last twenty years in these requirements? What sociological trends are reflected by this change?

6. Investigate the parallel history of child labor and required school attendance laws in your state.

7. What portion of your college's budget is allocated to vocational courses? Who controls the funding and budget of your college? How does this reflect the power of various groups interested in the program?

8. Compare income distributions in the census tracts of several high schools with the proportion of college-bound graduates in each. Does there seem to be a correlation? Many factors might cause such a connection. List as many as you can.

9. What changing patterns of employment have characterized your community in the last twenty years? How have vocational programs in the schools reflected this change?

BIBLIOGRAPHY

Boulding, Kenneth E. "The Schooling Industry as a Possibly Pathological Section of the American Economy." *Review of Educational Research*, XLII, 1 (Winter 1972), 129–42.

Burgess, Charles, and Merle Borrowman. *What Doctrines to Embrace.* Glenview, Ill.: Scott, Foresman, 1969.

Burridge, Trevor D. *What Happened in Education: An Introduction to Western Educational History.* Boston: Allyn & Bacon, 1970.

Carnoy, M. "Rates of Return to Schooling in Latin America." *Journal of Human Resources*, II, 3 (1967), 359–74.

Cave, William M., and Mark A. Chesler. *Sociology of Education.* New York: Macmillan, 1974.

Coleman, James, et al. *Equal Educational Opportunity.* Washington, D.C.: Government Printing Office, 1966.

Cremin, Lawrence A. *The Genius of American Education.* Pittsburgh, Pa.: University of Pittsburgh Press, 1965.

Goslin, David A. *The School in Contemporary Society*, Keystones of Education Series. Glenview, Ill.: Scott, Foresman, 1965.

Greer, Colin. *The Great School Legend, A Revisionist Interpretation of American Public Education.* New York: Basic Books, 1972.

Hall, G. Stanley. "Moral Education and Will-Training." *Pedagogical Seminary*, I (1892), p. 86. Quoted in Burgess and Borrowman, p. 64.

Howe, Harold, II. "Anatomy of a Revolution." *Saturday Review*. 20 November 1971, pp. 84–85, 95.

Jencks, Christopher, et al. *Inequality: A Reassessment of the Effect of Family and Schooling in America*. New York: Basic Books, 1972.

Katz, Michael B. *Class, Bureaucracy, and Schools, The Illusion of Educational Change in America*. New York: Praeger, 1971.

Mosteller, F., and D. P. Moynihan, eds. *On Equality of Educational Opportunity*. New York: Vintage Books, 1972.

Perkinson, Henry J. *The Imperfect Panacea: American Faith in Education, 1865–1965*. New York: Random House, 1968.

Polley, Ira. "What's Right with American Education?" *Phi Delta Kappan*, LI, 1 (September, 1968), 13–15.

Roszak, Theodore. *The Making of the Counter-Culture*, Garden City, N.Y.: Doubleday, 1969.

"U.S. Vocational Education Called Disastrous," *The Morning News* (Wilmington, Del.), 8 January 1975, p. 28.

Welch, Finis. "Relationships between Income and Schooling." *Review of Research in Education*. Ed. Fred N. Kerlinger and John B. Carroll. Itasca, Ill.: F. E. Peacock, 1974. II, 179–201.

Werdell, Philip. "Futurism and the Reform of Higher Education." In *Learning for Tomorrow, The Role of the Future in Education*. Ed. Alvin Toffler. New York: Vintage Books, 1974, pp. 272–311.

The Schools and the Integrating Function

	Individual in Focus	Group in Focus
Task		
Membership		Sanctions INTEGRATION Valuing

THE IMPORTANCE OF INTEGRATION

The social institutions of government and economics discussed in Chapters 2 and 3 focus upon the task functions involved in social interaction—government upon decision making, economics upon allocation. Functions in both these areas are readily observed. When a decision is made, the behavior of the group can be seen to change. Suppose the sixth graders decide to study India and go to the resource center. When an individual starts to work on his or her role in getting the task accomplished, something visible happens. Thus Sam will get out a book on the wild animals of India, the topic he has chosen.

Seldom is every member completely satisfied with all group decisions or even the task he or she is assigned. Naturally, then, conflict as well as cooperation arises when people join in groups. The resolution of these conflicts is important if the task is to be accomplished. In the group situation above, the teacher may say, "Stop fooling around, Sam, and get to work."

Chapters 4 and 5 focus on integration and socialization—the membership functions of groups. They are the equally important processes that serve to unite the group, keep its members working together, and mediate the conflicts that may arise. The membership functions of group processes are not so conspicuous as the task functions. They are less noticeable for two reasons. (1) Rather than being shown in specific unique instances, such as a decision made or a task undertaken, membership processes operate little by little over an extended period of time. (2) They are also characterized by being similar to a photographic negative; that is, the group is held together mainly by what its members do *not* do. Thus, Sam did not remain behind when the sixth graders went to the library.

Members usually conform in order not to be sanctioned or punished by the group. In terms of the life of a group or the majority of its members, sanctions are rarely invoked. The threat of them is enough to keep members doing what the group wishes. At the same time, most members share a common interpretation or explanation of what is normal behavior. They are committed to a common *ethos*, or set of values that distinguishes the culture of their group from the culture of other groups. These shared expectations pull a member to behave in the desired direction. The ethos can be conceived of as a glue that unites the members. Only a relatively small number of all possible human behaviors are identified as being acceptable and expectable. This is why what members do *not* do reflects a culture as much or more than what they actually do. Sam's teacher might not even have had to say, "Stop fooling around."

The *social integration* of the group—that is, the process of making a cohesive whole out of the many individual parts that compose it—is as necessary as the allocation of roles to get the task done. The role player has to stay with the group to get that job done. Sam must not switch his reading to model trains without good reason.

Since 1954 the word "integration" has usually been associated with racial desegregation. In its broader sense, however, the concept refers to all those processes that unify any system or structure. This broader sense is meant throughout the chapter.

The next chapter will describe how group expectations become internalized within members so deeply that individuals are frequently unaware of the original sanctioning that initiated the process. This dimension of the membership function, socialization, focuses on the individual. The behavior that the group wants is simply seen as "normal" by its individual members. What do you think Sam would have answered if you asked him why he went to the library?

Although integration (and its counterpart in individuals, socialization) is less visible, it is no less vital to the life of the group. In order to accomplish the task that brought the group together, the group must stay together until the job is done. Consider the Declaration of Independence. It begins by the most careful explanation of why the American colonial segment of the group known as the British Empire is going to break away: "A decent respect for the opinions of mankind requires that they should declare the causes which impel them to the separation." The Founding Fathers then proceed with a careful delineation of all the reasons that emboldened them to take the very dangerous step of leaving the group to which they had belonged.

A Brief History of the Techniques of Integration

Social integration is accomplished both by the subtle and covert influence of shared expectations and by the more visible process of *delivering sanctions*—forcing conformity to group norms. Although sanctions can be positive or negative, the methods animal and human groups have traditionally used to force members into an integrated whole have been negative. *Aversive control*, to use philosopher-psychologist B. F. Skinner's phrase for negative sanctions, might be a cuff on the ear from mama cat, a caning at the hands of the headmaster, or *ostracism* (expulsion from the group). The latter, derived from an ancient Greek practice, is the ultimate sanction for threatening the group's integrity. It works on the assumption that the life of the group is more valuable than the survival of a member who does not conform. If Sam doesn't conform, he may be expelled from school. The ultimate ostracism is capital punishment.

Two social agencies have had the power historically to deliver sanctions. In matters of government the state has the legal power to punish; in moral matters religious bodies can threaten punishment to their members—even the fires of eternal punishment in hell. Of course, both the state and the church also have the power to reward. But examples of this behavior are harder to identify.

The school's reciprocal function has been to inculcate in the young respect and support for law and religion as the proper institutions of society to deliver the sanctions the society has approved. Public schools have held Christmas programs. May 1 is celebrated as Law Day. Can you recall teachers being concerned over the use of profanity? Why should a public-school instructor be concerned with that?

The uniquely American invention, the common school, was expected not only to create good citizens and employment-ready workers, but also to act as a central agent in the "melting pot" of America. Such schools were to take members of all the diverse cultures that poured into our country and unite them in a common allegiance to the ethos of America. As late as 1967 James Conant, then president of Harvard University, was still calling for creation of a comprehensive high school, where pupils from all backgrounds would adopt a common belief in the shared values of American culture.

What is the ethos of the United States? Donald McKinley, viewing our industrialized society in 1971, saw the residual values of Puritanism: predestination, delayed gratification, and achievement as the sign of salvation. But as we now move into the postindustrial era, our shared values can be expected to change.

Schools were expected to inculcate the American ethos into

new members so well that the ultimate sanctioning power of law and religion would not have to be invoked. The school's task of inculcating support for integrating institutions was not simply to make the young aware that the law could throw them in jail, but to persuade them not to act in those ways that would result in jailing. Many middle-class youth, when arrested for illegal narcotic activity or shoplifting, are shocked when they discover that jail may be a real and possible result of their socially disapproved behavior.

Innovation in Social Integration

Two changes in methods of integrating members into society have occurred in the United States in the last fifty years. And once again, change suggests that the schools must be transformed if they are to continue to perform their reciprocal role with other social institutions.

One change has occurred in the historical integrating institutions. The force of organized religion has withered, and the authority of law is no longer considered to be unquestionable by large masses of youth.

At the same time, a new pervasive force for integration based on persuasion and subtle suggestion has overwhelmed American society, causing possible change beyond our present reckoning. This force is the impact of the mass media, particularly television, in establishing shared values. The mass media function by substituting the carrot of promised pleasure for the stick of negative sanctions.

This method of influencing human behavior has been shown by B. F. Skinner to be much more potent than the traditional methods of punishment and ostracism. Skinner calls the method *reinforcement*, which works by providing rewards for successive approximations of a desired behavior. (Strictly speaking, reinforcement and rewards are not exactly equivalent, though they are close enough to be used interchangeably in this context). Skinner believes that any animal—including all normal humans—can be taught to behave exactly as the "shaper" or "controller" desires. In a novel, *Walden Two* (1962), and a political essay, *Beyond Freedom and Dignity* (1971), he has described how we can integrate society by positively reinforcing socially desirable behavior. We could leave punitive sanctions behind us on the ladder of cultural evolution. Now we know how to pull new members toward desirable conduct by promising rewards rather than threatening force to push the individual away from illegal or immoral conduct. If we carefully planned to intentionally condition persons to operate in desired ways, we would need no stronger negative sanction than ignoring an unwanted response.

Paired with a belief that only quantitatively measurable behavior is worthy of a scientist's investigation, Skinner's theories have permeated much educational theory and practice. You will find his concepts referred to as reinforcement theory, operant conditioning, contingency management, and learning theory (although the latter also has other meanings). Skinnerian psychology forms the basis for many present-day innovations in education, such as *performance contracting, behavioral objectives,* and *competency-based teacher education*—terms that you will no doubt become familiar with as you progress in your education as a teacher.

The mass media cannot utilize the rigor of the scientist's definition of desired behavior, or measures toward it. But they share with Skinner an appreciation of positive reinforcement. The mass media utilize this attractive force by promising desired rewards, especially in advertisements. Negative sanctions are also sometimes suggested, such as becoming a wallflower if one does not use the proper mouthwash. The goals suggested by omnipresent commercial messages are essentially gratification of hedonistic (personal pleasure) desires. Hedonism combines with violence to drench programing in values that are directly antithetical to social cohesion. Little in the media encourages support of overarching group needs. Smokey the Bear's conservation campaign usurped little "prime time." And Smokey was unique in carrying the banner for shared concerns.

Schools can no longer simply inculcate common values already agreed upon by the society in general and enforced by church and state. Yet new members of modern society need to learn how to clarify and develop values that will be socially constructive as well as personally acceptable. We will reserve our discussion of how schools can aid the young to find such values until the end of the chapter. But first we will explore in more detail the relation of the school to the three main integrating institutions in contemporary society—law, religion, and the mass media.

THE SCHOOLS AND THE LAW

In Chapter 2 we discussed the relation of the school to the decision-making or legislative and executive branches of the government. This section focuses on the judicial aspect of government (though where possible we will show how court actions triggered legislative and executive action).

From the beginning of public schools, state and local courts and legislatures have made decisions that fostered conformity in schools; for example, laws have been passed and upheld concerning compulsory attendance, the sanction of corporal punishments, and teacher certification. Table 2.1 shows by the starred items the significant number of decisions by the federal courts that have influenced the conduct of school systems. Here we want to show the impact of court actions on two significant areas—civil rights and the legal rights of students and teachers.

Civil Rights and the Schools

In every society, but perhaps especially in a democracy, the rights and responsibilities of groups are frequently in conflict with the rights and responsibilities of individuals. Recent decisions of the Supreme Court to insure the civil rights of citizens have confronted established social habits that arose out of the integrating function of *social class*.

Social class may be considered an outgrowth of the allocations of the economic system, since money, specifically one's inheritance or wages, primarily determines one's social class. Class, however, also has an integrating function within society, since values held in common unite members of a social class and distinguish them from members of other classes. Children who enter private schools from the public system frequently have a period of social adjustment, especially if they are the first generation in their family to attend these more exclusive schools.

In traditional societies, one's membership in a dominant or subservient minority group also determines social class. The rigor with which an individual is confined to his social class as ascribed by his birth determines whether a class or caste system is in operation. A *caste system* prohibits individuals from moving out of their ascribed class roles. Neither achievement nor marriage will free members from the lifelong specific expectations of caste role. The "untouchables" of India are the most vivid example of caste ascription.

The institution of slavery in the first century of American life led to the establishment of a caste society for the black descendants of those who had been slaves. A similar caste status was also reserved by the white majority for American Indians and those Orientals who had been imported for cheap labor during the building of the transcontinental railroad. In order to keep these minority members integrated into their own caste, whites used many sanctions. A major one was the provision of segregated schools. Near the end of the nineteenth century, the Supreme Court declared that such schools were constitutional if while they separated they were also equal (*Plessy* v. *Ferguson*).

Nearly sixty years later, the Supreme Court reversed this decision in the landmark case, *Brown* v. *Board of Education of Topeka, Kansas* (1954). This case was also significant because it was the first case to be decided on an appeal to science rather than jurisprudence. The Supreme Court decision cited psychological research that suggested that segregation had a negative impact upon black children. This seemed to mean that schools could not be both separate and equal, since black children were being psychologically damaged by such discrimination. In striking down segregated schools, the Court struck down the major support of a caste system of social control in the United States.

The immediate impact of the *Brown* decision, however, was slight. The federal government had no financial leverage to back up the decision since it had not yet made a commitment to support the public schools financially. The executive branch did take some tentative steps to carry out the decision by calling out troops to enforce admission of a black man to the previously all-white University of Mississippi Law School and black children to the Little Rock, Arkansas, public schools.

Following the passage of the Elementary and Secondary Education Act of 1965 and numerous succeeding education bills, the amount of federal money allocated to schools became a ready force to discipline schools. If local schools or school systems did not follow federal regulations, these funds could be cut off and school services would be crippled quickly. School administrators had learned to rely on federal funds, especially for special and remedial programs. They did not wish to go without those funds, and they conformed for fear of losing them.

The Civil Rights Act of 1964 guaranteed that, if federal funds were used, the civil rights of persons of various races and religions had to be protected in schools. The Educational Act amendments enacted in 1972 extended the force of law by forbidding discrimination by sex as well as race or religion. This law prohibits the use of admissions quotas by sex or unequal expenditures for the salaries of male and female coaches or the teams they coach. All classes, including physical education, must be open to all students. Scholarship recruitment and aid must be on a sex-equal basis. What impact will that have on the college you attend? Or the school from which you graduated?

Once again, because funds may be cut from schools and colleges, conformity is protected by negative sanctions. Federal funds support libraries and laboratories, bus trips, and remedial reading, as well as peanut butter sandwiches at lunch time. As we noted in Chapter 2, positive sanctions such as federal funds for science programs also encourage nationwide school conformity.

The Legal Rights of Teachers and Students

Most human societies have an initiation rite, a point at which young members of society are accepted as full participants in the life of the society. Before that time, young members are considered not to be full citizens and under the control of the adult members of the group.

The Latin phrase *in loco parentis* (in place of the parent) has traditionally signified what the schoolteacher's role was to be in relation to the pupil. A teacher has been expected to take the same care for the safety and growth of a child as would a parent. On the other hand, until quite recently, he or she has usually been allowed to punish and chastise with the same freedom as would a parent.

Teachers have been sued for negligence in the care and safety of children, but the courts generally apply the same standard as they do to parents: "Was reasonable prudence used?" This applies only to teaching duties. Teachers are not responsible for the long-range health care of their students, for example. In the matter of gossip or public negative criticism of a child, however, teachers are liable for suits claiming defamation of character. Parents generally are not.

Children, on their part, have been expected by society to show respect for the adults in whose charge they are and to submit to the sanctions of school authorities as they do to the sanctions of their parents. Failure to conform with this expectation may lead to punishment within school, expulsion or suspension from school, or even to incarceration in a juvenile facility as "uncontrolled" or an habitual truant. Society makes it a crime not to attend school. And while in school, a pupil must behave in a socially acceptable manner. Some radical critics see this as oppression of children. (Norman Solomon, 1974)

In the 1960s a particular combination of circumstances led to a sudden upswing in nontraditional behavior on the part of students. Various student protests took place as a result of the pressures for civil rights and in protest against the Vietnam War. Many young people felt the war was an illegal activity since it had not been declared by the Congress as required by the Constitution. In nonviolent action, youth began to wear armbands as well as long hair as a sign that they protested or rejected the society which they felt was acting immorally. And at the same period, youth began to use narcotic drugs, which were forbidden even to the adult members of society.

Both mild and extreme forms of behavior that were deviant from previous expectations brought legal actions against youth. A rash of cases went to the courts questioning everything from the school's right to sanction dress codes to the legality of unannounced locker searches. Case by case was decided in favor of a student's rights to freedom of expression and movement. Freedom from illegal searches and seizures, guaranteed to adults under the Bill of Rights, was extended to youth. In the words of *Tinker* v. *DesMoines Independent Community School District,* "a student's rights do not stop at the school yard door." Nowadays a student may not be expelled from school without some kind of juridical hearing. This most frequently takes place before the Board of Education acting under its third power of decision making.

These court decisions have swept away many of the expectations of traditional conformity. Court decisions in many cases have supplanted the interpretations of state and local boards. Even the *in loco parentis* role is being questioned as school administrators and teachers struggle to establish new methods of determining which pupil behavior may be sanctioned and which may not. Courts can be expected to support school rules that are reasonable and relevant to learning. But the days of the arbitrary authority of schools and teachers over pupils are gone.

THE SCHOOLS AND RELIGION

The tie between these two great institutions of human society goes back to preliterate society. Primitive tribes established groups we would identify as schools, especially in order to teach the rite and rituals that the practitioners of primitive religion needed to know. Choir schools in the Dark Ages of Europe kept the learning of the ancients alive by training youth to chant the ritual of the Christian churches. As European civilization was reborn in the Renaissance, the demand for a highly educated clergy inspired the establishment of many universities. The Protestant Reformation stressed the need for believers to have access to the Bible, and schools were established that all might learn to read the Holy Word.

During the colonial period in America, schools were sponsored by the established (state-supported) churches. "In Adam's fall, we sinned all," begins the alphabet poem of the eighteenth-century New England primer. Little Puritans learned their values with their ABCs.

Many schools sponsored by the Episcopalians and Presbyter-

ians were founded in the revolutionary period. Young gentle-
men could no longer sail to the mother country to receive an
education proper to their station in life. As private academies
and boarding schools, many of these institutions have continued to provide training for members of the upper classes in
American society. Others of these institutions became private
colleges, most of which have since abandoned their formal connections with these religious sects.

Members of other Protestant sects resented the educational
dominance of the wealthier Episcopalians and Presbyterians
through these church-affiliated schools. They therefore supported the establishment of public schools. The Constitution
called for the separation of these state-supported common
schools from any religion. What followed provides a vivid example of how a group's shared perspective causes its members
to expect one behavior as normal and to bitterly sanction those
who will not conform:

> In 1848 in Protestant Massachusetts, for example, it was possible
> for Horace Mann to note with pride that the Bible (the King
> James version), "the acknowledged expositor of Christianity,"
> was being used in the common schools by common consent at
> one and the same time he emphasized the importance of nonsec-
> tarian instruction. (V. T. Thayer, 1970, p. 109)

Protestant hymns and prayers permeated school functions.
And all seemed "normal" as well as nonsectarian "since many
Protestants saw the school as only one in a network of agencies
—including family, church, Sunday school and tract society—
through which they sought to attain their educational social
goals." (Douglas Sloan, 1973, p. 258)

Then began the mid-nineteenth-century immigration of Roman Catholics—the Irish, the Italians, and the Poles among
them. Those Protestant hymns, prayers, and the King James
Bible were not their norms. They petitioned that their children
be excused from these expected behaviors.

Catholic children were threatened, whipped, and expelled.
The courts supported the common schools in these sanctions.
Things grew so bad that in Philadelphia "riots in 1844 resulted
in the deaths of perhaps a dozen people, the injury of many
more, the burning of two Catholic churches, a seminary and

over forty other buildings." (Robert Potter, 1967, p. 229) Not surprisingly, as discussed below, Catholics soon withdrew to schools of their own.

For one hundred years, however, the Protestant aura surrounded public schools. Protestant prayer and readings from the King James Bible traditionally began each school day. Twelve years of classes terminated with a baccalaureate service in which the graduates were prayed over by the local pastor and exhorted in a sermon to go forth as moral as well as political adults. Rarely was a rabbi or Roman Catholic priest invited to deliver the baccalaureate sermon.

Not until 1962 did the Supreme Court acknowledge the Protestant dominance of the American public-school system. Then, in two decisions, the hand-in-hand relationship of meetinghouse and schoolhouse was torn apart. In the case of *Murray* v. *Curlett*, the Court ruled that in public schools no secular authority could prescribe one form of religious expression in preference to any other. And in *School District of Abington Township (Pa.) et al.* v. *Schempp et al.* (1963), Bible reading and daily prayer were banished from the school room, and religious services under the aegis of the schools were forbidden. Any such activity the Court held to be "an establishment of religion, contrary to the First Amendment."

Subsequently, school and legal authorities agreed that our cultural heritage encourages teaching about religion in social studies classes and that the "Bible as literature" is an acceptable English unit. The previous close interaction of two mutually compatible agencies, church and school, however, was severed so far as public education was concerned.

Parochial Schools

Roman Catholics, when spared the violent reaction of Protestants to their nonconforming children, still naturally enough did not see the public schools as a place where they might be sympathetically received. Further, it was the desire of many immigrant groups to retain both ethnic and religious identity. Many parents wanted to give their children a special religious education, which the Constitution forbade (at least so far as non-Protestants were concerned).

So in 1884 a meeting of the Catholic hierarchy at Baltimore

called for each parish to set up a school for its children. Thus was established the school system that in 1970 educated one out of every eight elementary students. In states where many Roman Catholics reside, as much as 25 percent of the school-age population may attend parochial (parish) schools.

The education that these schools provide the youth who attend them differs from the education of Catholic boys and girls who attend public schools according to Andrew Greeley and Peter Rossi, who made an extensive survey of the education of Catholic Americans in 1966. Although this influence interacts with the influence of family characteristics and the length of time pupils attend parochial schools, boys and girls in parochial systems tend to achieve a higher socioeconomic status upon graduation than do Catholic children who attend public schools. Further, graduates of Catholic colleges who have also attended Catholic parochial schools show differences in values from other Americans. "Those who attended Catholic colleges are not only significantly more 'liberal' than Catholics who did not, they are, on the measure of anti-Semitism, significantly more 'liberal' than college-educated Protestants." (Greeley and Rossi, 1966, p. 225)

While education within a religious context appears to have caused this difference in values, Greeley and Rossi found that parochial school graduates are no less well integrated into the melting pot of American culture than are their coreligionists who graduate from public schools. On measures of community activities, friendships outside their own religious subculture, and general tolerance, Catholic children do not differ depending on where they attend school. Greeley and Rossi developed an interesting hypothesis for the greater achievement of Catholic graduates of parochial schools which we shall review in Chapter 6, "The Structure of the American Public School."

With a high proportion of young people enrolled in Catholic schools, there appear to be several effects on the public-school system. By providing a visible and articulate alternate educational system, the Catholic power structure exerts considerable influence on public-school supporters. For example, many non-Catholic parents, in their complaints about lack of discipline in the public schools, cite the stricter control that characterizes parochial education. Sometimes this makes public-school officials (who are accustomed to a monopoly in educational expertise) nervous. They may be inclined to act while glancing over their shoulders for an anticipated response from the religious educators.

Parents and the public who support by fees and church assessments their own educational system traditionally are less interested in the quality of the public system that they must simultaneously support. Like the childless senior citizens, they do not wish their taxes increased to support a system from which they obtain no particular benefit. Thus the tax money and public support available to public schools may be seriously limited in areas with a high percentage of youth enrolled in parochial schools. (Peter H. Rossi and Alice S. Rossi, 1957)

The Roman Catholic schools have played a unique role in the racial desegregation process in the United States. They have consistently refused to be the refuge for whites fleeing Southern desegregated schools. The Church of Rome has long enrolled both blacks and whites in Southern schools and maintained traditional middle-class schools in the heart of black ghettos, to which both whites and blacks might go. This may be contrasted with the Southern Baptist Church and other fundamentalist Southern Protestant sects that have established private schools for whites throughout the South following the desegregation decision.

The enrollment in other religious and private schools combined constitutes only a tenth of the population of those involved in Roman Catholic education. The latter system therefore still comprises the major alternative to American public schools.

Until 1950 Roman Catholic parochial schools were supported by tuition fees and a general parish assessment. Taught by religious nuns and brothers who had taken the vow of poverty, Roman Catholic schools could operate much more cheaply than public-school systems. In the 1960s and 1970s, however, many religious teachers began to leave their church-school posts, and lay persons had to be hired to replace them. The laity needed adequate salaries, and, at the same time, school costs were rising even more quickly than did other costs of living, so the budgets to support Catholic education suddenly increased abruptly and dangerously.

The predominantly Protestant culture of the United States used the doctrine of separation of church and state as a reason to withhold federal funds from parochial schools. Monies were delayed a decade because of pressure from the National Education Association. This organization of public-school teachers feared that money spent on children enrolled in parochial schools would weaken the near monopoly of public education and thereby weaken the power of public-school teachers. Finally, in the Elementary and Secondary Education Act (1965), a compromise was reached by which parochial students would receive federal funds directly. Church-school officials were bypassed as the funds flowed through the administration of the overlapping public-school systems. In this way Catholic children received the benefits of increased funding as did pupils in public schools. On the other hand, this method of funding ostensibly prevented a religious institution from acquiring property or personnel or using federal funds for a religious purpose. The state also kept control and accountability for the tax monies so allocated. (George Killen, 1970)

As costs continue to rise, one may expect further pressure to increase support to pupils in nonpublic schools. The courts have declared that schools other than those publicly established are indeed constitutional. Pupils in private schools may now be transported in buses run on tax-raised dollars. Parochial schools with educationally disadvantaged youngsters may receive federal funds comparable to those dispersed to public schools with similar pupil populations.

Much of the interest in the voucher system as an alternate form of educational support comes from persons involved in religious schools of diverse faiths. What arguments can you see for and against the public support of schools whose main purpose is education in a religious context?

THE MASS MEDIA AS INTEGRATING AGENCIES

As we noted earlier, the mass media have become a powerful new institution for integrating society. Nationwide film, radio, and television programs present vivid representations of what a modern society considers "normal" behavior. Joining the formal pronouncements of bench and pulpit, the mass media overtly purvey values of current socially expectable behavior. What gives these media their particularly forceful and generally uncontrolled impact, however, is the subtle, almost covert communication contained below the surface of the ostensible message. What appears to be merely an automobile commercial also informally supports values regarding property, materialism, and an entire life style. Only recently has the tremendous power over our social expectations of these truly "hidden persuaders" (as sociologist Vance Packard refers to them) been recognized. Currently, American society is struggling to find a proper control over these new integrating agencies.

Pamphleteers like Thomas Paine, who ignited the American Revolution, had an impact upon a small group of influential readers in the days when the written word was the major means of communication. In the last fifty years, however, motion pictures, radio, and television reach millions in a moment with messages that are far more powerful.

The propaganda films of Nazi Germany were one of the first conscious manipulations of public ethics via the media. Hitler's power was derived in part from his spellbinding radio speeches and mass meetings, filmed and projected in movie houses all over Germany. Some students of communication wonder if the German people thus came to support values, such as the persecution of Jews, which, as individuals reading reflectively or in discussion with others, they might never have adopted otherwise.

A Canadian college professor, Marshall McLuhan, has drawn attention to the difference in the nature of the impact of the mass media in a series of books beginning in the mid-1960s. Essentially McLuhan believes the electronic media have an immediate emotional or feeling impact, as opposed to the intellectual influence of printed materials. The message comes by way of the medium of communication. According to McLuhan the world has become like a "global village," in which attitudes and ideas are transmitted with the speed of back-fence gossip. (McLuhan and Fiore, 1968) One night in 1974 a late-night TV show host jokingly referred to a shortage of toilet paper, and within a week supermarket shelves were emptied across the whole United States. Apparently the nation's anxiety over the "fuel crisis" spilled over into this area, and thousands, though spread over hundreds of miles, acted as one integrated mob as they hoarded the "scarce" commodity.

As important as the medium may be, the messages conveyed by the mass media in the United States are having an impact upon the integrating values of our society. By implication, these are the values that ought to be adopted if a new member is to be successfully integrated into adult society. Just two examples will underline the power of the media.

Television brings into the homes of the poor the reality of what life is like with a moderate to high income. The subtle message of TV is that the life pictured on the screen is the normal way of living in America, which may immediately be compared to the standard of living of the home viewer. Never has such an incentive for redistribution of wealth been laid before the poor. Many social scientists saw this overt visualization as the spark that ignited the revolution of "rising expectations" eventually provoking the urban riots of the 1960s and 1970s. Charles Reich, in his famous book *The Greening of America* (1970), sensed the power that the *covert* message had upon the middle- and upper-class youth who also rioted on campuses across America. They too had viewed on TV our society's definition of the "good" life and yet they who were supposed to be experiencing it found the reality existentially barren and unfulfilling. In the words of Walter Lippmann," A self-indulgent generation in large part is an unhappy one. We are very rich, but we are not having a very good time." (Quoted by James Reston, 1974)

As the troubled decade of the 1960s drew to a close, President Lyndon Johnson asked ex-President Eisenhower to lead a study commission into the causes of violence that had swept across the United States. Among other social forces, the commission pointed to the purveying of violence as a normal social response in innumerable television programs. (Robert Baker and Sandra Ball, 1971) Ten particularly violent television shows were taken off the air in 1969. But in 1970 a special report by the Surgeon General of the United States pointed to the fact that *children's* programs were "still by far" the most violent on the home screen. (Cited in William Melody, 1973)

In addition to the values and expectations that the programs themselves convey, other subtle messages are put across, particularly in the commercial advertisements that financially support the programs of the major television networks. As we noted above the appeal here is almost exclusively to individual and immediate gratification, for that is what sells products. Hedonism and violence are behaviors that tear at the fabric of society. Few groups can survive without some sacrifice of individual desire to the needs of the group as a whole and without a rein upon the aggressive drives of the human animal. Indeed, civilization is characterized by societies that control these antisocial impulses. Only intermittent and infrequent public service announcements point to the good of the whole nation or society amid the jungle that has been called a "wasteland."

And who has been most drenched with these messages—most unable to check them against the truth of real life?

> There has been a growing realization of the tremendous impact television has on the acculturation process of the young. Statistics on the amount of time children watch television compared with time spent in school or even sleeping, and the volumes of other research on the effects of the medium on children, increasingly demonstrate that television's overall impact on children is a topic that cannot be dismissed lightly. Although television is in many instances replacing the role of the traditional institutions such as schools, family and church, in children's lives, it has been relatively free of the legal and moral constraints that are imposed on the other institutions in their dealings with children. (Melody, 1973, p. 84)

Because of the commercial support of most broadcasting, social controls upon radio and television run up against constitutional guarantees of freedom of the press and an individual's rights to utilize personal private property as one wishes. Self-policing by the broadcast and film industries has resulted in the relegation of violence to hours when children are supposed to be in bed or to movies rated PG, R, or X.

But public policing can bring the United States dangerously close to government-managed news. This, in fact, occurred during the crises of both Vietnam and Watergate. Pressures at these times came directly from the executive branch in the White House. The official organ of government control is the

Federal Communications Commission, which, like many other regulatory agencies, is weak because of the ties of its members to the very industries they are supposed to be overseeing. Nevertheless, Lawrence Cremin argues:

> The Federal Communications Commission is already in the business of making educational policy in the United States. It carries some of the classic responsibilities of a school board and that being the case, it ought to employ genuine educational criteria in making some of its decisions. (Cremin, 1965, p. 106)

Citizen efforts to encourage the FCC to play such a role have coalesced around church groups. ("What Can We Do?" 1975) Religious organizations in this way may maintain a role in the integration of American society.

Little evidence exists that schools have subjected the products of electronic communication to the rigor of analysis used upon the traditional print media. Yet statistics indicate that children, by the time they graduate, have spent more hours before TV than in school.

The mass media display the values of personal pleasure, materialism, and instant gratification. Schools, on the other hand, traditionally have been expected to inculcate the values of public service, personal worth derived through work, and postponed gratification. It is probable that any conflict of values within the children is minimal, because television portrays the rewards of its value system much more vividly than do the schools. What transformation is required here? At least two educators believe that schools must adopt the more subtle— and more enjoyable—teaching techniques of the media:

> Education and entertainment have long been treated as separate categories of experience, despite the efforts of philosophers and psychologists to make clear that learning can be enjoyable. It may be that the most revolutionary consequence of the greater availability of learning made possible by the newer media will be to demonstrate universally that learning never has to be painful, that good teaching can be as enjoyable as the best entertainment. From the standpoint of the learner, given a choice between learning that is enjoyable and learning that is not, it is not likely that inherited beliefs would stand in the way of enjoyment. (Peter Rossi and Bruce Biddle, 1966, p. 370)

And if the schools ignore the competition of the media—fail to make education more enjoyable—what would happen to them? The same educators have this to say:

> Insofar as schools lost their local monopoly status (in education) through competition with commercial media, they would also lose much of their basis for controversy over curricula, architecture and student conduct. Those who differ could go elsewhere; education would become as free as book publishing.

THE SCHOOL AS SOCIAL INTEGRATOR

In return for legal and moral support to the schools, the educational establishment has traditionally been expected to inculcate youth with attitudes supporting the values that hold society together and make it operate efficiently: a common culture from a common school. In Chapter 3 it was suggested that school taught young workers-to-be the work-oriented values of punctuality, fulfilling responsibilities, and perseverance—vocationally valuable skills in an industrialized society.

Like the media, the methods as well as messages of school convey social values. Schools rate an individual's worthiness by grades and ranks, crowning the most work-successful as the valedictorian of the class. Donald McKinley cites this practice as a reflection of the Protestant ethic that success in work equals the ultimate success (salvation) of an individual. (McKinley, 1971) Waiting for a year-end grade, waiting for graduation, waiting for an adult job to crown your scholastic efforts—all these school goals train young people to postpone their rewards and gratifications as they are traditionally expected to do in a civilized society.

Schools are supposed to nourish the basic ideas of democracy, such as the principles that no person is above the law and that the minority should bow to a majority decision. Frequently curriculum materials are expected to convey the moral imperatives. (Remember "In Adam's fall," etc.?) School rituals of pledging flag allegiance suggest expectations of national loyalty and patriotism.

What happens when there is a change of values in the society as a whole? As an example of what may happen in a period of rapid cultural change, consider the turmoil that surrounded the introduction of sex education courses into some schools. As well as attitudes toward sexual morality, this struggle, caused by changing social values, brought to the surface political and racial attitudes. The John Birch Society, a right-wing political group, took on many new members when they opposed materials advocated by the Sex Information Exchange Council of the United States (SIECUS). (Mary Breasted, 1970) Many strident voices were raised against any sex education in some schools, and the tax support of schools was threatened in some communities. This tendency for changes in value education to roil public-school supporters is the reason James Coleman believes public schools usually keep clear of value conflicts in society. As public institutions, they are expected to be "neutral," purveying only those values that all members of society can be expected to adopt. (Coleman, 1966)

What has been the nature of the schools' response to the conflicts in social values that have torn this country apart since the 1950s? Different schools have, of course, responded differently. But it seems clear in most cases the response was not self-initiated by the school personnel themselves.

Expressed simplistically, some segments of society determined that other drugs in addition to alcohol should be socially accepted, and the schools responded with more health facts in science classes; the civil-rights movement brought minorities nearer the mainstream of American society, and schools introduced classes in black history; Vietnam resistance split the country, and schools permitted students to participate in school-sponsored Moratorium Day assemblies. But who initiated these responses? Black militants with their white cohorts, parents scandalized at drug arrests in school corridors, students deeply distressed over their lives being endangered by a "peacetime" draft. The schools reacted to intermediating forces; they seldom acted in direct response to the actual solid changes. Perhaps the response of a school superintendent addressing his teachers on "Classroom Implications of Watergate" well exemplifies the nature of the schools' usual response: "First, I think we need to teach the history of our country as it reveals the need for a free press and free speech. This concept should be a part of our social studies program at all levels." (Katz, 1974, p. 465) In terms of the transformational model, we might say the schools assimilated changes on pressure from outside their system (in this case, Watergate) but little accommodation was made in the schools' traditional way of doing things (teaching abstract concepts in a social studies class).

In addition to the overt teaching of values such as patriotism, what values are taught covertly in our schools? Some educators have identified a "hidden curriculum," which selectively reinforces the values of the status quo. Because the hidden curriculum fits so smoothly into the expectations of the majority, it is almost invisible, hence hidden. The nineteenth-century religious sectarianism of the common school was such a covert value. But the hidden curriculum also operates more subtly. For example, the arrangement of seats in a classroom suggests implicitly whether pupil needs or teacher authority determine what learning is to take place. Could you diagram this? It sometimes takes the equivalent of a classroom with no chairs to make visible the significance of the hidden curriculum.

One of the major ways in which schools inculcate values is not through overt ritual or even the hidden curriculum, but rather through the conscious modeling of acceptable social behavior by teachers. In *The Sociology of Teaching* (1932) William Waller identifies this aspect of the teacher's role as the "model citizen." Because of their high visibility in the community and the power they hold over the young entrusted to them, schoolteachers have traditionally been expected to reflect what the community sees as the best moral behavior. Psychological research supports the fact that children learn values by imitating a model with which they wish to identify. It appears this may be one of the most potent methods for instructing youth.

What happens when teachers display a model of immorality, such as patently lying? For example, in many states, as a condition of employment, teachers must sign an oath to uphold the federal and state constitutions and laws, one of which may prohibit public employees from striking. Children staying home from shut-down schools hear via radio and television that 400 out of 600 teachers in a system simultaneously called in sick. Further, they know that when a state legislature refused a teachers' wage increase, the teachers' union promised not a strike but a "concerted job action."

> Schools have been a primary force in the individual's induction into the norms and values of society, and it has been the duty of the teacher to inculcate the ideals of democracy, fair play, respect for authority, and obedience to legitimate rules. Teachers who participate in strikes or boycotts, which are forbidden by state law, may forfeit a certain amount of respect from both students and the public. Their image as models of good citizenship is difficult to reconcile with strikes and tends to increase antagonism among school board members, administrators, and the general public. (James Guthrie and Patricia Craig, 1973, pp. 18–19)

As the country moves from an industrial to a postindustrial society, as cultural diversity replaces a common system of values, conflict between a variety of contemporaneous value systems will mark our society. What should the schools do? Is their only choice either to maintain an intransigent and reactionary insistence upon the values of a daily more outmoded status quo or to abandon a disciplined and concerted effort to create moral individuals? There is a third alternative that may help to transform society as well as the educational institutions themselves.

Ethical behavior is marked by a consistency of choices among means to reach an overarching end. Youth can be taught methods of clarifying the values by which to choose one possible future over another kind of future, one set of means in preference to another. Rationality and direction can be brought to bear on the legions of choices each modern person must make.

Three trends in values education are now coming together to suggest a new approach to social integration. From philosophy, Louis E. Raths (1966) has identified a series of teachable processes for personal value clarification. This approach has been adopted by many groups working in the "humanistic psychology movement," that (in contrast to B. F. Skinner and other behaviorists) focuses upon self-understanding and self-motivation as the key to improved social interaction.

A more traditional psychological approach is recommended

for all classrooms by psychiatrist William Glasser (1969). From his work in "reality therapy" with emotionally disturbed children, Dr. Glasser has developed methods of improving the emotional growth of normal children. His special contribution is the premise that an individual must accept responsibility for his actions as opposed to excusing one's behavior due to "circumstances beyond one's control."

Based on the cognitive psychology of structuralist Jean Piaget, Laurence Kohlberg has identified stages in the development of moral learning. This permits a more specific tailoring of the curriculum and expectations of moral development. This clarification brings value education into the scientific realm of the empirical and accountable. Kohlberg's ideas have been useful in a variety of situations. Growth in moral understanding has been shown among members of a wide variety of groups in and out of schools. (James Rest, 1974)

There is no guarantee that knowledge alone will make one wise. The earliest empirical studies of morality by Hartshorn and May in 1927 illustrated a since well-documented psychosociological fact: persons may *know* what is morally expected, but given a particular set of circumstances, there is no guarantee they will *behave* morally. On the other hand, to thrust young people into the present stream of conflicting moral currents with no techniques at all for establishing a set of moral channel markers (even if the channel may shift) is to guarantee they will be swept first this way, then the other, by propagandists and purveyors of special interest.

Learning how to value well—not expediently but wisely—is a skill central to survival for both individuals and any democratic society. Teaching this skill should be a central task for public schools in today's world.

MAIN IDEAS

1. Religion and law are the traditional institutions of social integration.
2. Schools have been expected to inculcate values that support the concept and sanctions of law and religion.

3. Change has occurred in the schools' integrative function because of a decline in the influence of law and religion and a rise in influence of mass media as an integrating force.
4. Civil rights decisions and legislation have balanced the integrative force of social class membership by upholding the individual rights of citizens.
5. The 1960s saw a greater emphasis upon the rights of students. The unquestioned authority of the school was broken by legal action.
6. Public schools, though constitutionally prevented from union with any sect, have consistently promulgated Protestant values and rituals. But recent court actions have curbed this influence.
7. Rising costs indicate more public support is needed if alternatives to public schools are to survive.
8. Roman Catholic schools provide the major alternate source of education in the United States.
9. The mass media, because of their vividness and immediacy, now persuade Americans what values are expected by modern society.
10. The schools' role as a social integrator must be changed to allow for changes in the values of society and a shift in power from religion and law to mass media as the major source of value dissemination.
11. Specific attention to values education is required if students are to be free and responsible in their choice of modern morals.

GLOSSARY

behavioral objectives Description of learning goals using activities that may be empirically validated.

caste system A social class system in which individuals are prohibited from moving out of their ascribed class roles.

competency-based teacher education Preparation of professional skills based on behavioral objectives.

delivering sanctions   The process of forcing group members to conform to the norms of the group.

ethos   The common interpretation and expectation of certain behaviors as "normal," accepted as basic values by a culture.

ostracism   To be pushed or kept out of a group.

performance contracting   Division of learning objectives into segments of behavioral objectives that a pupil contracts to learn or an educational agency (other than the school) contracts to teach.

reinforcement   Pairing a preferred outcome with a desired behavior in order to cause the behavior to recur. A popular translation is "to reward," although Skinnerians make a distinction, since by ignoring behavior it may be negatively reinforced.

social integration   Processes that make a unified social system of the many individuals or small groups brought together by a common task.

social class   A subsystem within society sharing the same cultural values and usually the same economic status.

SUGGESTED ACTIVITIES

1. Compare and contrast several theories of classroom control. "Contingency management" or "operant conditioning"—two terms for control by Skinnerian methods—should be included. (You might wish to use methods of reinforcement to see if you can change the behavior of another.)

2. Review the history of legal requirements for teacher certification in your state. What trends do you note? What relation have they to trends in the larger society?

3. How does the law define the relationship of student and teacher in your state? May a teacher or administrator physically punish a pupil? What are the insurance regulations that protect students from teachers, and vice versa?

4. Arrange a day's visit to a parochial (not necessarily Roman Catholic) school if you are a public-school graduate (and vice versa if you went to a parochial school). You will observe ob-

viously different behaviors—the presence or absence of public prayer, for example. But what other, more subtle differences do you note in, say, textbooks or curriculum?

5. Analyze the purveyed values in an evening's worth of TV programing and commercials. Watch Saturday morning children's programs. What values does society present to its new members here?

6. Discuss with a radio or TV station's ad department what brakes, if any, they put on commercial program messages. Ask about "freedom of the press" and what they feel about their station's relationship to the Federal Communications Commission.

7. Interview English supervisors, coordinators, or teachers about lessons in evaluating the product and values of the electronic media. How are these lessons the same or different from those focusing on printed materials?

BIBLIOGRAPHY

Baker, Robert K., and Sandra Ball. *Violence and the Media*. Staff Report to the National Commission on the Causes and Prevention of Violence. Washington, D.C.: U.S. Government Printing Office, 1971.

Breasted, Mary. *Oh! Sex Education*. New York: Praeger, 1970.

Coleman, James, et al. *Equal Educational Opportunity*. Washington, D.C.: U.S. Government Printing Office, 1966.

Conant, James B. *The Comprehensive High School: A Second Report to Interested Citizens*. New York: McGraw-Hill, 1967.

Cremin, Lawrence. *The Genius of American Education*. Pittsburgh, Pa.: University of Pittsburgh Press, 1965.

Glasser, William. *Schools Without Failure*. New York: Harper & Row, 1969.

Greeley, Andrew M., and Peter H. Rossi. *The Education of Catholic Americans*. Chicago: Aldine, 1966.

Guthrie, James W., and Patricia A. Craig. *Teachers and Politics*. Bloomington, Ind.: Phi Delta Kappan Educational Foundation, 1973.

Katz, Malcolm. "Classroom Implications of Watergate." *Phi Delta Kappan*, LVI, 8 (March 1974), 465–67.

Killen, George A. "Federal Aid to Private and Parochial Schools, An

Analysis." *The Bulletin of the National Association of Secondary School Principals,* 347 (September 1970), 88–100.

McKinley, Donald G. "The Ethos of Industrial America." In *Society and Education: A Book of Readings,* 2nd ed. Ed. Robert J. Havighurst et al. Boston: Allyn & Bacon, 1971, pp. 2–11.

McLuhan, Marshall, and Quentin Fiore. *War and Peace in the Global Village.* New York: Bantam Press, 1968.

Melody, William. *Children's Television: The Economics of Exploitation.* New Haven, Conn.: Yale University Press, 1973.

Platt, John. "World Transformation: Changes in Belief Systems." *The Futurist,* VIII, 8 (June 1974), 124–25.

Potter, Robert E. *The Stream of American Education.* New York: American Book, 1967.

Raths, Louis, et al. *Values and Teaching: Working with Values in the Classroom.* Columbus, Ohio: Charles E. Merrill, 1966.

Reich, Charles A. *The Greening of America.* New York: Random House, 1970.

Reston, James. "Developmental Psychology as a Guide to Value Education: A Review of Kohlbergian Programs." *Review of Educational Research,* XLIV, 2 (Spring 1974), 241–59.

Reston, James. "Lippmann's Credo in His Own Words." *The Sunday Bulletin* (Philadelphia), 15 December 1974, section 2, p. 2.

Rossi, Peter H., and Bruce J. Biddle. *The New Media and Education.* Chicago: Aldine, 1966.

Rossi, Peter H., and Alice S. Rossi. "Background and Consequences of Parochial School Education." *Harvard Educational Review,* XXVII, 3 (Summer 1957), 168–99.

Skinner, B. F. *Beyond Freedom and Dignity.* New York: Knopf, 1971.

Sloan, Douglas. "Historiography and the History of Education." *Review of Research in Education.* Ed. Fred N. Kerlinger. Itasca, Ill.: F. E. Peacock, 1973. I, 239–69.

Solomon, Norman. "On Confronting Ageism." *Edcentric: A Journal of Educational Change,* 30 (June–July 1974), 12–16, 27.

Thayer, V. T. *Formative Ideas in American Education from the Colonial Period to the Present.* New York: Dodd, Mead, 1970.

"What Can We Do?" *Between the Lines,* XXXIV, 2 (15 January 1975), 4.

The Schools and the Family

	Individual in Focus	Group in Focus
Task		
Membership	→ By Family ← SOCIALIZATION → By School ←	

THE INSTITUTIONS OF SOCIALIZATION

A basic attribute of the human animal is the long time it takes a human infant to become able to survive independently. It is estimated that in a nonhostile environment, with adequate and easily obtained food, a baby would probably not be able to survive alone until at least five years of age. No other animal needs so long a period of infant dependency simply to survive.

Because of this biological fact of life, human beings have as a basic social unit the *family*. Anthropologists nowadays define the family as a child and a nurturing adult, usually the child's biological mother. Because of the relative physical weakness of the female and her preoccupation with the care of the child, it is frequent that a male member of the human tribe takes on the protection of the mother and her child. But, as we shall discuss further below, this is not a universal pattern by any means.

Human children remain in the family group for many years past the first five needed for basic survival. There are many more tasks for a modern human to learn than how to make one's way to the grocery store and back. These tasks are generally defined as socialization, previously defined as the process by which the human animal learns to become a member of the groups to which he or she belongs by birth or acceptance. In the family the established norms of society are taught to the young, and they learn that they ignore these norms only at some danger.

Recent research on the higher apes and humans indicates that for any anthropoid infant to grow into a fully functioning adult, early nurturing must include cuddling and comforting, not just provision of food and physical safety. "Warmth" is the word used by our culture to describe this essential social environment. The emotional climate of the family drenches the young in an atmosphere that develops in them socio-emotional needs for acceptance and approval by other human beings, especially by the adult humans who control food and safety, as well as providing "warmth." In later groups to which humans belong, they continue to need socio-emotional support.

In respect to socialization, schools, as we noted in Chapter 1, are an outgrowth of the family. The schools' job is to continue the socialization process initiated in the family group. The family is ultimately responsible for this process, however, and parents are held accountable by law for providing their children with an education.

So historically and ultimately, the primary function of schools is to socialize new members into the ways of the group, to continue the family process of passing on the socially established ways—"normal" behavior. Citizenship education, job training, an education in value, are simply aspects of the one most basic task—to make group members out of human individuals by modifying the self-centered baby animal into a socially sensitive adult. In our society the maximum development of individuals is valued, not least because that is seen as bringing maximum benefit to the group through increased contributions to it from fully realized individuals. The truth of this statement may be recognized more clearly if you consider what sanctions are put on extreme individual behavior that is not perceived as beneficial to society.

Schools have assumed an ever larger part in the socialization of modern youth because of the greater complexity of modern technological society.

> Education has become increasingly specialized and professionalized. The result has been a widening gap between the parent and the teacher in respect to presumed if not actual technical expertise, and a transference of more and more responsibility for at least the formal educational aspects of socialization from the family to the school. (David Goslin, 1965, p. 91)

The interrelationship between schools and this other major social institution, the family, is then in as much a state of transformation as are the relationships between the school and the social institutions discussed in Chapters 2, 3, and 4. Once again, there is a need to transform schools in order to react to this change in the social system as a whole.

Three Aspects of Socialization

The concept of socialization is so all-encompassing (from where to find a mango tree to using a laser to mend a detached retina) that behavioral scientists have tried to break down aspects of the concept into smaller units of consideration. In Chapter 1, we presented a brief analysis of three aspects of the concept—culture, enculturation, acculturation. Here it would be useful to review and expand upon these terms so that we can understand the weighty task society has given to the family and the schools.

These three aspects of socialization are tied up with human beings' long period of dependency. To understand their relation, you must first understand the two reasons behind a child's long dependency.

First, the human animal simply takes a longer time biologically to fully develop *after* being born, rather than completing most development prenatally. Simple organisms begin life in the same form and with the same functions as adults of their species. But the complex organism we know as modern man living in today's technological society may take as much as a fifth to a fourth of a normal life span getting ready to live as an adult. Children in school are changing before our eyes, simply because the biological release mechanisms are still ticking off various surges years after humans have emerged from the womb. The various strains of adolescence that affect youngsters in the high-school years are vivid examples of school-children exhibiting the extended developmental period of the human animal.

The second reason for the extended period of human dependency is that man has so much to learn—modern man especially. To pluck a mango from a tree requires very little learning, once one knows where the mango grows. To locate a grocery store in a new town, to identify what brand of mango juice is best, and to pay and accept the proper change are very much more complex. Travelers in a foreign country where not even the alphabet used is the one they learned may struggle to survive. They are suddenly very aware of the portion of behavior that derives from having learned a method of operation—behaviors that were not in their "repertoire" as a result of birth or physiological development.

Humans have certain common problems they must solve regardless of the society in which they live; the acquisition of food is a good example. But *how* they solve these problems varies from society to society. Those behaviors that each society selects as the way it will solve the common problems make up the culture of that society. Culture is the constellation, the complex interwoven web, of all those learned behaviors that each society says is the "right" or "normal" way for its members to behave.

In Chapter 4, we discussed the attempt of society to make individuals accept these norms as their own norms. This socialization process is enculturation. As suggested in the previous chapter, it may be that the schools are going to have to take a greater responsibility for this aspect of socialization.

Historically, however, the schools have been more concerned with the process of acculturation, which deals with the transmission of the learned behaviors of culture from one generation to the next. The curriculum defines what society thinks it is important to pass on to new members so that society will survive. This may include the interpretation of the flight of birds as an augur of well or ill for the empire, the irregular French verb, the sayings of Chairman Mao, or the hypothesis that $E = mc^2$.

Out of the great attic storehouse of all that human beings have learned and passed down by word of mouth, by picture, and by written word, each society selects for its schools' subject matter what it feels its members need to know. Nothing more quickly spells the doom of a society than when the wrong selection is made or when no new selection is chosen when the environment of that society creates a new situation.

There is so much we can learn—the very magnitude of it is bedazzling. But what must be selected and taught without failure to our youth who will live out the majority of their lives in the twenty-first century? We will take on that question toward the end of the chapter, but first we must describe more fully the factors that influence the process of cultural transmission.

FAMILY INFLUENCES ON THE SCHOOL

It has been said that all children bring their families to school with them. What they bring are two effects of the five years of family socialization that have molded their earliest existence before they enter the schoolhouse.

One of these effects is the subculture to which a particular child's family belongs. The culture of modern America is further divided into subcultures—ethnic, religious, class, geographic, and other subunits each solving the common tasks of survival in American society in slightly different ways. The family imprints upon the newborn the specific norms and expectations of the subculture(s) to which the baby's family belongs. For example, in our society aggression must be inhibited and exhibited only under selected circumstances. Some subcultures permit the child to exhibit aggression in the home, but not against outsiders. Other groups reverse this, permitting aggression against nonfamily persons but prohibiting its expression toward immediate kin.

The child brings all these prohibitions and expectations of his or her "kind" (and a definition of who is included in the classification "kind") to school. Does the student's ethnic subculture have a history of success or failure in the American school system? How does this affect his or her personal expectations?

The second school-important factor that the child brings from home is a view of himself or herself as developed through these early intrafamily relationships. The socio-emotional environment of the home in those early years leaves an image in the child's mind of his or her acceptance, lovability, and power to control the future. The sociologist Carlton Combs spoke of "the looking glass self," that self we see reflected back to us by the people around us in the way they speak and act toward us. Our self-concept develops from our relationships with others, most particularly those significant others that make a difference in our life's fortunes.

Both sociologists and psychologists point out that the processes of our earliest socialization have particularly potent impact upon our lives for several reasons. First, they are primary, laid down with no competition from previous learning. Second, they are perceived and projected in a socio-emotional, as opposed to a rational or cognitive, mode: their meaning is not available for verbal understanding. Finally, they deal with the core (the self-concept) of personality in relation to people (parents) with godlike power over the small individual.

The first lessons of socialization then are stamped in with an intensity no school can match or probably challenge without the supportive involvement of the child's very first teachers—the parents. In fact, reinvolvement or continuing involvement of parents may be one clue to improving the self-expectations of students. Since a student's expectation appears to be the key to student success, we will examine this further in a later part of this chapter.

Subcultural Impact upon School Experiences

It is difficult to distinguish between those aspects of a student's behavior caused primarily by a family's particular cultural environment and those that result from his or her own self-concept. This is particularly true when we focus on the expectations the student has for personal success. But bearing this in mind, we shall look first at subcultural effects, and then turn to family impact upon the individual's self-concept as distinguished from membership in a subculture.

Subcultures, as we have noted, can be divided in a number of ways by any distinguishable criterion. There exists, for example, a subculture of bowlers and one of ballet fans. Sociologists speak of *variables*. Most sociological research has tried to measure the subcultural variables of class, race, and religion. Each of these factors has a relation to the others that is known scientifically as *interaction*—the influence of one variable on another that results in combined behavior different from the separate effects of each. For example, much research identified membership in the Roman Catholic religion as bringing about certain behaviors, failing to note that family size and (in the United States today) economic class are also associated with membership in the Roman Catholic Church. Was faith alone producing characteristic behavior, or was behavior caused *also* by the two related variables? To find out, social scientists would have to bring the *uncontrolled variables* of family size and class (uncontrolled because their possible impact was not considered by experimenters) under study.

One of the most difficult interactions in our country is that of race and class. What behaviors of children in the black ghetto result from their participation in black culture, what from their environment of poverty? What from the interaction of the two variables? One study seems to indicate that at the lowest economic level, conditions of poverty may make blacks and whites respond similarly. But in the middle class, race makes a significant difference in response. (Steven Tulkin, 1968) In other words, the relationship between these two variables may not always be constant, or the same. If we change the value of one, we cannot accurately predict the other will change in a similar manner.

At the moment in sociology, the state of the art is such that we know subcultural differences influence school-children, but we are just beginning to unravel the tangled skein of the many threads of these influences. The task is further complicated because, in addition to the complex interactions of various subcultures, the way the subcultures' impact on school performance is delivered is also important. We have been able to identify three separate ways that have some influence:

1. The attitude of the culture toward schooling, thought to account for the auspicious success of Jewish and Japanese children in the American public-school system
2. Whether the home is intellectually impoverished or enriched—the so-called cultural deprivation variable (Are there books in the home? Does the child have a quiet place to study?)
3. What knowledge the child has of the "student role" (Has the youngster learned how to behave in the classroom? Has he or she learned to wait for rewards?)

Research on subcultural factors has concerned itself with each of these influences and with a variety of subcultural combinations.

It is important to emphasize here that whether a particular subcultural variable will actually have an influence depends upon how active other subcultural influences are. To take a simple example, the Greek restaurant owner who says that he and the Jewish owner of a pawnshop are the "only foreigners" in an isolated rural town identifies with a different subculture than if he lived in a nearby city with several Greek churches and social clubs. In this Greek's case, rural subculture (specifically, his alienation from it) is more significant in influencing his behavior than the ethnic subculture of being a Greek-American.

Because of the massive immigrations to the United States in the nineteenth century, the ethnic-religious subcultures of America have appeared to have more discernible impact upon school-children than do the subcultures of different generations, or of rural-urban-suburban differences. More research has been focused upon measuring the impact of these ethnic-religious subcultures than others that may be even more important.

Differences in the socio-emotional climate of homes have long been suspected of influencing school success. In the middle of this century, that is, roughly between 1930 and 1960, much research about differences in child-raising techniques was focused upon the variable of social class. Early results seemed to indicate that lower-class parents trained their children to value security as opposed to risk-taking and getting along as opposed to getting ahead. The opposite values were thought to be inculcated by middle-class parents. Thus each class appeared to prepare its children for the role they would probably play in the world of work. But the mass media spread a common cultural expectation during this era, and it now appears that such differences no longer differentiate the child-rearing practices of the lower and middle classes. (Urie Bronfenbrenner, 1958)

Following the *Brown* decision of 1954 and the "Great Society" legislation of the Johnson era in the mid-sixties, concern was expressed for what was identified as the "cultural deprivation" of poor children, especially poor black children. Various programs in what was called "compensatory education" were instituted to make up for this assumed deficiency in preparing children for the school. A. Harry Passow, reviewing compensatory education programs in 1974, found that such measures largely failed to equip lower-class children with an equal opportunity in the American public schools they presently attend.

Many of these programs focused on the concept that lower-class families did not sufficiently verbalize with children to prepare them for the talky world of the school. Yet Doris Entwistle found that "slum children are apparently more advanced linguistically than suburban children at first grade." (Entwistle, 1970, p. 14) Apparently something happens soon within the school to blunt this early natural head start in language arts. Perhaps it is the school that is deprived in its inability to utilize and capitalize upon the strength of language and expectation that lower-class children bring.

You will recall from Chapter 3 that various studies have revealed that differences in school achievement seeming to reflect racial differences may in fact be attributed to income or class differences. The most important variable in school achievement is the subculture of economic class of the majority of parents in a school. If it is predominantly middle class or better, students will achieve. If it is predominantly lower class, children will fall behind.

As Figure 5.1 shows, with a student's sex, the socioeconomic status (SES) of a family has a multiple and complex impact upon student academic performance. Sociology has not yet discovered what valences, or measures of strength, to attach to these lines of force. Like the relation of class and race, there is no guarantee that a general formula applicable to a majority of students will be found. As noted before, however, one researcher, Christopher Jencks (1972), believes that family SES alone is sufficient for predicting future vocational success and is associated in greatest part with success in the present school system.

Figure 5.1 Characteristics of Individual Students Related to School Performance

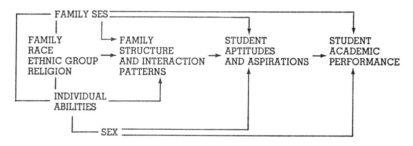

SOURCE: Sarane S. Boocock, *An Introduction to the Sociology of Learning.* Copyright © 1972 by Houghton Mifflin Company. Reprinted by permission of the publisher.

While the various subcultures of religion, geography, age, and ethnic background condition a child's ability to succeed in the American school system and thus to be socialized into mainstream America, the socioeconomic class of the child's parent remains the single most important subcultural value. This influences an individual's personal success in school in the fashion outlined in Figure 5.1. Equally important, at the same time, is the SES of other families in the neighborhood. This determines the school's influence, tax base, public support, and the facilities of staff and plant. The child born into a middle-class family in a middle-class neighborhood is almost guaranteed success; in contrast, a child born into a low-income family in a low-income area is probably going to fail in his or her effort to use the American public-school system as a key to success and personal growth.

This fact is so patently undemocratic and in opposition to our vision of the American public school that it is hard to accept. But until we do accept this reality, we cannot begin to identify what we can do to change it and thus transform the schools into the sources of equal opportunity that we say we mean them to be.

Self-Concept Impact upon School Experiences

More and more research data is beginning to point to the very significant impact a pupil's view of himself or herself has upon future success in school. Such a view is called the child's *self-concept*. If a child comes to school with an expectation of success in school and in life and manages to *maintain* that expectation, his or her achievement moves upward with that expectation. The child who comes to school expecting failure, or whom the school soon teaches to fail, will watch achievement slip with his or her expectations.

The subcultural impact upon expectations and achievement discussed in the preceding section focused on the family system's interrelationship with the human environment in which the family is embedded. An individual child's own self-concept is first constructed from relationships within the close internal structure of the family. Here is where the child first learns what reaction he or she is most likely to provoke by certain behavior; from these lessons a picture arises of how the world "out there" will respond to personal efforts. Much of this learning takes place on a nonverbal level. It has a very high emotional component and has proved very hard to modify in the very verbal but much less emotionally intense environment of the school.

Sociologists view the development of a self-concept as that constellation of individual behaviors at the center of a variety of roles that a human being learns to play in various social settings. Figure 5.2 presents a model of this.

In the family a small male child learns about himself from

Figure 5.2 Self-Concept Pictured as Role-Generalized Behavior

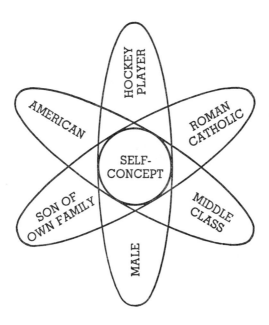

playing the role of mother's son, and father's son, and perhaps Grandma's boy, and sister's brother, and dog's companion, and the annoyance of the old man across the street. After five years of this extensive training, he comes into the schoolroom to learn new roles and be further socialized. But the pattern is already very much determined as to how these and other subsequent role behaviors will be developed.

The school may be the child's first introduction to a task-oriented, formal group. For the first time he or she is expected to behave with little respect for his or her own feelings but with much respect for people and institutions that have no primary personal importance. This is a jolt in social expectations some children find very difficult.

Social scientists have isolated a number of factors influencing the self-concept a child develops. Four of these factors are variations in family structure, sex role expectations, birth order, and child-rearing practices.

Variations in Family Structure. The most important person to each human being in that earliest period of almost complete helplessness is the person who plays the nurturing role. In most animal societies (including that of humans), this role is played by the female who gave birth to the baby. Among the higher primates, including man, a male frequently assumes the protection of the nurturing mother and her newborn in return for services rendered by the female. But as mentioned in the introduction to this chapter, there are many varieties of family structure. The "typical American family" of married male and female pair with their two or more natural children is not by any means a universal pattern, even in the United States. Such a family, with its intense mutual dependencies, is called a *nuclear family* because it contains the "nucleus" of a wider system of kinship relationships. This nuclear pattern has developed within the last 150 years of Western civilization as a result of the mobility, both geographic and economic, brought on by the Industrial Revolutions.

Before the forces of technological change brought about this form of family structure, European countries and their American colonies were more likely to be organized into an *extended family* structure. In this sort of family, several generations and degrees of kinship share the family labors and hearth. Talcott Parsons explained the development of the nuclear family as an adaptation resulting from the stresses and strains of the multiple roles a highly technological society demands its members play. The tight structure of the nuclear as opposed to the extended family provided a protected environment where the young could learn this variety of roles without too much danger of early failure.

The American public-school system traditionally expects that its students will come from nuclear families. Boys and girls who come from single-parent homes have been subject to considerable research to see what effect this may have upon their success in school. A 1965 presidential advisory commission concluded that fatherless homes were devastatingly debilitating. Black children from single-parent homes were seen as irremediably handicapped in competing in the American school system and economy. Black boys especially were thought to suffer in what were called "father-absent homes."

They had no male model after whom they could pattern their masculine role behavior. So went the theory. (Daniel Moynihan, 1965)

Recent research has indicated that once more it is not a simple relationship of one to one. Consideration must also be given as to whether or not the major breadwinner in the family is employed. Children whose father is in the home, but unemployed, showed poorer student performance and attitudes than did students of working mothers without a working male present in the home. Sarane Boocock (1972) suggests that the key appears to be whether the males and females in the home are playing the roles that society generally assigns. This means the father is expected to work, but the mother may or may not do so. Given an employed father, whether or not the mother works appears to have little impact on her children's success in school.

Most recently, the extended family has been cited as a better preparation for school success than the nuclear form. (John Biggs, 1974) As we move into the postindustrial era, it may be that the nuclear family will cease to be the most socially useful form of nurturing new members of our society. Some other structure, such as multiple-parent families, may turn out to be a better training ground for the socialization of the very young.

Sex Role Expectations. American society has traditionally assigned separate, complementary behaviors to males and females. Boys are expected to be aggressive; they are given toy soldiers. Girls are expected to be nurturing; they are given dolls. Children have learned how to play adult sex roles by identifying with the adult males and females they see in their homes.

Part of this expectation has been that males succeed in school and work and females do not. In American schools in the last hundred years, girls have surpassed boys in achievement until the dating years. Then boys pull ahead, or girls lag behind, or both patterns of behavior occur. So in high school and college, we see a reversal of the early pattern: males surpass females in achievement and vocational success. Much of the thrust of the women's liberation movement is toward reducing the vitality and impact of these sex-linked expectations. Techniques to accomplish this vary from efforts to enforce the Educational Act of 1972, which prohibits discrimination on the grounds of sex, to programs that underscore sex bias in elementary reading primers.

Nowadays, there are many examples of what Rhona and Robert Rapaport have called "the dual career family." (1969) The young dual career couple suffers strains from role conflict (Who prepares the meals at the end of a mutual working day?) and personal identity crises (Shall he give up his job when she gets a better one 500 miles away?). In the important early years of career advancement, they also have to decide whether to have children and how to allot responsibility for nurturing them. These are new but endemic problems in our society. In the future, males will undoubtedly be involved in child rearing; probably more women will be sole breadwinner.

We may expect that these changing methods of sex-appropriate behavior may influence girls as they are growing up, so that they come to see themselves as persons who can achieve and have worth in society independent of their relationship to a status-holding male. You might speculate on what will happen to the self-concept of males as female expectations change.

Birth Order. Expectations of success have also been related to the order in which a child is born into a family. But once again we have identified a variable that may or may not be scientifically *significant*, that is, attributable to a cause other than chance. Whether it is depends upon many other factors, such as the family's social class and age of the mother when the children are born. Clearly, the first-born of middle-class white families usually show a higher need for achievement, which is translated into real vocational success. All American astronauts, for example, are either first-borns or only children. More lawyers are first-borns.

On the other hand, in a lower-class family, the youngest child may be the most highly motivated. And in a small family children born when the mother is younger have higher achievement than their siblings; but when the number of children increases, those born when the mother is older are liable to have a higher desire to achieve.

Child-Rearing Practices. Reference has been made to a child's expectation of success, or of his or her "need to achieve" (nAch as it is symbolized). This last phrase represents an identifiable dimension of personality, which can be measured with a good degree of predictive success by the time males are teen-agers. (J. W. Atkinson, 1964; David McClelland, 1961) We know that high scores on nAch characterize white middle-class males. Boys without this attribute may have high ability but will be poor school achievers. Some research has related this to child-rearing practices by mothers. Early training creates in sons the desire and the expectation that they can and will succeed on tasks of moderate risk.

It would be helpful if this clue to achievement: (1) could be extended to females; (2) could be extended to members of other social classes; (3) could be reliably tested at an earlier age and so possibly modified during the school years. Unfortunately, none of these conditions is presently possible, and the need for achievement joins many less well-defined or testable attributes in the collection of clues we have about the relation of child rearing to school success.

We do have other research-provided clues about the nature of this relationship, though one study showed that nurturance (defined as a sense of family "closeness") appears to differentiate children who remain in school as opposed to those who drop out. (Lucius Cervantes, 1965) Another study of families who lived in five different countries (and therefore, of course, five different cultures) indicates that excessive parental authoritarianism is related to early school leaving regardless of the cultural environment of the family. (Glen Elder, 1965)

Other research has focused less on these emotional or affective descriptions of parent-child interaction and looked instead at parental styles in verbalizing and using various levels of cognitive development in dealing with children. The significant question in this research is, How much do mothers "explain" or answer a child's searching questions? (Robert Hess and Virginia Shipman, 1965)

The number and complex interactions of all these variables of parent behaviors are additionally affected by the reaction of children to these behaviors. The individual development of each child's self causes idiosyncratic responses that make each parent-child relationship even more unique.

When teachers set out to modify (hopefully to raise) a child's sense of competence and expectation, getting parents involved seems mandatory. At the end of each school day, the student is again immersed in the family's way of operating. An entire range of parent behaviors may have to be modified if a child is to change in a significant fashion. For such a total system approach, we need to work with the entire family unit, not just the child. In a 1969 study Wilbur Brookover and Edsel Erickson found that parental involvement was the key in their extended effort to raise students' expectations of success. "Having to go to school for Johnny" can have a new positive significance.

THE CHANGING ROLE OF THE SCHOOL
AS A SOCIALIZING AGENT

Earlier in this chapter we noted that the school's traditional task of socialization has been to pass down from generation to generation those things that a society sees as needed for its survival, that is, cultural transmission. This knowledge includes not only how to play various roles in that society, but also some of the tools and information needed for playing these roles. The most needed tool in every modern culture is basic literacy—the three Rs, if you will—and others are added to that according to the needs that a particular society envisions.

But now we may be entering a new era. Our most famous anthropologist, Margaret Mead, suggests that previous generations had no dreams of what our world and the world of the future will be. A curriculum based on what Mead calls "postfigurative" cultural selection—a selection based on what was needed to survive in the past—may equip our youth to live in the nineteenth century, but we exist in the twentieth. Mead believes that today we are educated by our peers—what she calls "a cofigurative" cultural selection. This education is occurring primarily outside the schools, within the popular culture, where TV, films, and songs instruct the youth in what they now need to know in order to survive in the present.

However, the twenty-first century is dawning, and this era calls for "prefigurative" cultural selection—not by our parents or our peers, but by our children, who Mead believes see more clearly what lies ahead. (Mead, 1970)

Societies, and modern societies especially, do not all move forward in time smoothly. One piece (usually the technology) leaps ahead, and the other institutions are pulled along. When one or more institutions are behind, sociologists speak of *cultural lag*. Mead's interpretation of modern socialization suggests a double lag. Some of us are listening to our peers, but the schools are still listening to our forefathers.

Ever since John Dewey's concept of the child-centered school was misinterpreted to mean, "Do I have to do what I want to do today?" educators have been sensitive to suggestions or criticism that children are establishing their own curriculum. Surely we adults have something to contribute to the socialization of these new members of our society; surely they couldn't do it better solely by themselves!

Adults do retain a charge to acculturate the young, though perhaps the task is different from simple cultural transmission. Suggestions for changing the focus are discussed in the following chapters, and previous chapters have suggested that teaching students to learn how to decide, how to learn, and how to value may become increasingly important. But the task most clearly associated with the word "socialization" is "learning how to relate." In present and future years, there are likely to be two aspects to this: (1) learning how to relate to other human beings, and (2) each individual's learning how to relate to his or her own self-concept.

The preceding discussion about self-concept underlined how schools are in a position (when working with families) to raise or lower a child's self-concept, to make it more realistic, more healthy. Especially because one's view of one's self now appears to be so integral to how well one achieves, schools are focusing much more specifically on activities that have an impact upon a student's self-concept. They are undertaking this effort not only to make children more at one with themselves, but also better to accomplish the school's traditional responsibility to acculturate the young.

Comparing life in a modern technological society with that

of a simple primitive society, vast differences in the nature of human relationships are clear. For example:

1. We have many more relationships during a lifetime as well as at any single time.
2. We have more interaction with persons of different backgrounds and perspectives.
3. These relationships are much more temporary; few, if any, last for a lifetime.
4. Fewer religious or class restrictions structure the form of the interactions.

Because of these trends, citizens of the future will need to become much more skilled at more rapidly establishing, nurturing, and letting go the innumerable human relationships into which they will enter.

What Social Relationships Do Schools Teach Today?

In discussing the impact of family factors on student learning, we emphasized that the family's view of the usefulness of schooling had an effect on the child's achievement. One way we have apparently convinced many lower-class families (and their children—our pupils) that the American school system isn't useful is by an expectation that all children should share the middle-class values that the majority of teachers bring to school.

The success of the American school system in tracking children into unskilled jobs has resulted in part from the ability of many teachers to impress upon lower-class children that they cannot succeed in public schools. One needs no fancy, scientifically questionable studies (Robert Rosenthal and Lenore Jacobsen, *Pygmalion in the Classroom*, 1968, for example) to demonstrate this; a strict comparison of drop-out rate, grade failure, and SES will offer proof.

The traditional classroom social structure teaches children to relate to teachers in a submissive, unquestioning way. Social or intellectual creativity represents a threat to most teachers since they perceive their job as transmitting an agreed-upon curriculum. Students and teachers generally have to reach the graduate level before exploring new knowledge as a part of their education.

The popular culture is rich with phrases that have been invented to describe what happens in classrooms. "Apple polishing" and "buttering up" are two of the more polite phrases for techniques of social manipulation schools teach children to use upon persons in authority. Students learn to scorn "teacher's pet" and to deride "the scapegoat" upon whom all their classroom frustrations are heaped. Possibly the absence of matching positive expressions reflects a linguistic convention toward euphemism.

Competition for grades "on the curve" teaches the lesson, "I can succeed only if you fail. Some of us have to get D's if some are to receive A's." Sometimes we hear, "You can't be a very good teacher if everyone passes with high marks." These attitudes of submission, stifled creativity, and success through competition represent the heart of the hidden curriculum discussed in Chapter 4.

In fairness other more positive social relationships are frequently taught in schools: teamwork, good sportsmanship, taking turns, relinquishing individual gratification for the good of the group and responsibility for public property and younger members of the school society. But they coexist uneasily with the ones mentioned above.

How Might Schools Teach Social Relationships Tomorrow?

Every daily paper or monthly magazine underlines our present concern that we need to improve more our skills in social relationships than our skills in manipulating machinery. They tell us that

> —the threat of an earth-annihilating World War III does not arise from our inability to master weaponry.
> —within nations, class and racial conflict is apparently increasing, or at least the violent expression of it are.
> —personal relationships are at present shallow and transitory.

The need is great. How will the schools respond?

When the great drug crisis of the early 1970s hit the American school system, students taught the teachers that the root of the matter was a sense of spiritual impoverishment and that "drug facts" taught in the traditional manner were not the cure. Successful teacher in-service drug education was focused upon improving relationships between students and students, between students and teachers. Schools discussed whether or not they wished to improve social relationships. Time and effort were required. That meant something else in the curriculum had to go. Some schools are still reluctant to release nineteenth-century studies for the consideration of twentieth-century problems. But if a school does see its responsibility to foster skill in human relations, there are a series of identifiable steps for teachers to take.

First, we know that not everyone is equally gifted in teaching in this area. It may even be that those who respond more to their subject matter than to their students ought to be excused from this arena and left to teach what they teach best—"learning how to learn."

Second, old or new staff members engaged in human relations training for students probably ought to begin with an understanding of their own behaviors and motivations in dealing with others. Are such lessons merely thinly disguised opportunities to manipulate students in an even more insidious way than the old teacher-is-boss techniques?

Third, teachers can be taught techniques for developing improved understanding of others. J. William Pfeiffer and John E. Jones, for example, have edited a four-volume handbook (1974), containing over a hundred "games" that can be used to improve understanding, communication, and group growth. Other methods include some of those mentioned in our discussion of values education in Chapter 4.

Lastly, there is an apparent need to discover ways of making "others" significant or real to us. Because human animals need the approval of others toward their behavior, their behavior can be modified by enlarging their view of who may be concerned with that behavior.

Recent research, for example, suggests that students vary their behaviors from situation to situation according to the persons who are "significant others" to them within each situation. Thus parents' aspirations are dominant in academic behavior, even while approval of peers is most significant in social relationships. The human animal has the ability to select from his many personal interrelationships those that are most significant to him at the moment he is involved in a specific task. (Brookover and Erickson, 1969, pp. 71–75)

On three social levels—the international, national, and personal—modern Americans have yet to learn how significant some others are when making decisions. This is perhaps the oldest problem known to man for the human animal strives first for his own self-preservation and only later, in becoming socialized, considers others. Internationally, Americans need to have others in famine-threatened lands become real. Hard choices are going to have to be made in allocating dwindling petroleum resources between petrochemical fertilizer, which increases crop yield, and the gasoline that automobiles demand. Nationally (in slicing up national wealth) Americans need to become sensitive to the fact that members of other classes have needs as real as their own.

Most basic of all may be the impact of casual sexual and marriage relationships. Failure to consider others in these most basic human relationships threatens the mental health of the youngest members of our society—the children.

Education for Family Living. Many schools have taken up a concern for improving interpersonal relationships, especially as they relate to family life. The managing-a-budget lessons of all-female home economics classes have been expanded to include both young men and women, and a far wider curriculum of concern. Unfortunately, classes like these too often bear the onus of being thought of as "sex education" or "frills" by highly vocal and active segments of the society. The expertise provided by real professionalism may counterbalance these forces. And it seems essential they be overcome.

The human animal remains a creature with an extended period of dependency. Physical dependency is closely interwoven and eventually transcended by emotional dependency. In the most immediate face-to-face group, which we may define as the family (no matter how structured), these dependencies are lived out and become the base for our deepest subsequent relationships to mates, friends, and our own children.

The existential despair of unrelatedness, identified as ano-
mie, springs from emotional deprivation in earliest childhood.
The human animal needs to be cherished and held in order to
become fully realized. As humans advance technologically,
child rearing assumes greater and greater importance in producing a fully realized human being who is able to be compas-
sionate and sharing.

Today many male-female relationships—within or without
marriage—result in unsought for, unwanted children. Religious sanctions for their responsible care have weakened.
These children frequently cannot find love from other members
in an extended family. Children of separated parents are
passed from hand to hand, back and forth, both parents wish-
ing to be rid of their burden. Statistics on child abuse mount.

Since the family is the frame within which the psychological
nurturing of adults takes place, schools bear a responsibility to
aid future parents in realizing the significance of the "others"
(children) who will be involved as the parents pursue their
individual gratification. This is a fundamental task for personal and group survival. In this way, the circle of socialization
can be closed, with the parents preparing children for school
and the school preparing children to be parents.

MAIN IDEAS

1. In order to be fully human, the human animal must be
   taught to live in human society. This process is called
   socialization.
2. Schools are an adjunct to the family, which is the social
   institution primarily charged with socialization.
3. Socialization involves:
   a. Culture—the matrix of all learned behaviors that a
      society says is right or "normal" for its members to
      exhibit
   b. Acculturation—the initiation of the individual into
      the facts and skills his society values
   c. Enculturation—the adoption by an individual of the
      norms of a society as his or her own
4. The family influences the school:
   a. by the subcultural norms it teaches a child

      b. by the self-concept it helps a child create

      c. by its desire and ability to support the school

5. All of these factors interact in a highly complex pattern of influence.

6. In producing successful school achievers, variations in family structure appear to be less significant than stability and emotional climate.

7. If a school is to improve achievement, it must improve the required variable of expectation of success. To do this, parents must be involved more vigorously than heretofore.

8. The school's traditional role in socialization has been the transmission of culture, or the acculturation, of its students.

9. There is a lag between the culture the school has been teaching and what today's students will need to know to survive in the future.

10. In the mobile and transitory society of the future, members must be able to relate meaningfully with others.

11. Learning how to relate is a socially valuable skill to teach.

12. Schools are moving toward an emphasis upon relating students to a positive self-image because of an increasing appreciation of its necessity in achievement.

13. Many schools have taught a hidden curriculum of social relationships based on submissiveness, lack of creativity, and self-aggrandizing competition.

14. Schools can teach improved relationships between nations, between groups within a nation, and between individuals.

15. There is a special need to create future parents who will be responsive and caring toward the new human beings who are developed physiologically and emotionally under their care.

GLOSSARY

This chapter perhaps more than those preceding it approaches sociology from the perspective of a behavioral science. The discussion derives from research data that has attempted to relate student behaviors to a variety of social-psychological factors. Scientific terms that are used are marked by an asterisk.

cultural lag The gap that exists when one social institution progresses and the others do not

extended family A family made up of many generations or relatives.

family Most basically, an infant with a nurturing adult. There are numerous variations of this basic unit in the wide range of human societies.

*interaction The combined force of two or more variables that results in effects different from the force of both considered individually.

nuclear family Male and female parents with one or more children.

self-concept The view that a child develops of himself or herself by playing a variety of roles in various settings.

*significant variables In statistics, a conclusion that a variable has influenced results with an impact greater than chance.

subcultures Divisions of the culture along ethnic, religious, class, geographic, or other differences. Each division represents a cohesive unit solving common tasks of survival in slightly different ways.

*uncontrolled variable A condition that may have an impact upon results but that has not been accounted for by the experimenter.

*variables Specific conditions that have different values under different circumstances.

SUGGESTED ACTIVITIES

1. Investigate the developmental theories of Jean Piaget. A good secondary source is Mary Ann Spencer Pulaski, *Understanding Piaget: An Introduction to Children's Cognitive Development* (New York: Harper & Row, 1971).

2. Review recent issues of *The Journal of Marriage and Family Life* to see what concepts are currently receiving attention in this area of sociology.

3. Discuss with a school psychologist, home visitor, nurse, and/ or social worker what techniques schools use to improve communications with families.

4. Interview a lawyer or caseworker with a local family court regarding their views on changing family relations and the role of the school in socialization.

5. Some communities have social agencies particularly focusing upon family problems. What services are available in your community?

6. Select a specific religious, ethnic, or class subculture and investigate what impact it is thought to have on educational achievement.

7. Interview a variety of members from one subculture about their attitudes toward schools and education. What similarities and differences do you note among them?

8. Investigate what changes in the family system are suggested in the literature of women's liberation and of the counterculture.

9. List what activities at a school known to you reflect a hidden curriculum. Can you identify whether its tenor is positive or negative in improving social relationships?

10. Read Abner J. Peddiwell, *The Saber-Tooth Curriculum* (New York: McGraw-Hill, 1939), a satire on education.

11. With a trained counselor, utilize some of the techniques from *A Handbook of Structured Experiences for Human Relations Training* (see bibliography). What is your evaluation of their efficacy and suitableness in various school settings?

BIBLIOGRAPHY

Atkinson, J. W. *An Introduction to Motivation.* Princeton, N.J.: Van Nostrand, 1964.

Biggs, John W. "Family Structure, Educational Mobility: A Cross-Generational Approach." *The Division Generator*, IV, 3 (May 1974), 3–8.

Boocock, Sarane S. *An Introduction to the Sociology of Learning.* Boston: Houghton Mifflin, 1972.

Bronfenbrenner, Urie. "Socialization and Social Class Through Time and Space." In *Readings in Social Psychology*. 3rd ed. Ed. E. E. Maccoby et al. New York: Holt, Rinehart and Winston, 1958, pp. 400–25.

Brookover, Wilbur B., and Edsel L. Erickson. *Society, Schools, and Learning*. Boston: Allyn & Bacon, 1969.

Cervantes, Lucius F. "Family Background, Primary Relationships and the High School Dropout. *Journal of Marriage and the Family*, XXVII (May 1965), 218–23.

Elder, Glen H., Jr. "Family Structure and Educational Attainment." *American Sociological Review*, XXX (1965), 81–96.

Entwistle, Doris. "Semantic Systems of Children: Some Assessments of Social Class and Ethnic Differences." In *Language and Poverty: Perspectives on a Theme*. Ed. F. Williams. Chicago: Markham, 1970.

Goslin, David A. *The School in Contemporary Society*. Glenview, Ill.: Scott, Foresman, 1965.

Havighurst, Robert J., and Bernice L. Neugarten. *Society and Education*. Boston: Allyn & Bacon, 1967.

Hess, Robert D., and Virginia C. Shipman. "Early Experience and the Socialization of Cognitive Modes in Children." *Child Development*, III and IV (1965), 869–86.

Jencks, Christopher, et al. *Inequality: A Reassessment of the Effect of Family and Schooling in America*. New York: Basic Books, 1972.

McClelland, David. *The Achieving Society*. Princeton, N.J.: Van Nostrand, 1961.

Mead, Margaret. *Culture and Commitment: A Study of the Generation Gap*. Garden City, N.Y.: Doubleday, 1970.

Moynihan, Daniel P. *The Negro Family: The Case for National Action*. Washington, D.C.: Office of Policy Planning and Research, U.S. Department of Labor, 1965.

Passow, A. Harry. "Compensation Instructional Intervention." In *Review of Research in Education*. Ed. Fred N. Kerlinger and John B. Carroll. Itasca, Ill.: F. E. Peacock, 1974. II, 145–75.

Pfeiffer, J. William, and John E. Jones, eds. *A Handbook of Structured Experiences for Human Relations Training*. I–IV. San Diego: University Associates, 1974.

Rapaport, Rhona, and Robert N. Rapaport. "The Dual Career Family." *Human Relations*, XXII (1969), 3–30.

Rosenthal, Robert, and Lenore Jacobson. *Pygmalion in the Classroom*. New York: Holt, Rinehart and Winston, 1968.

Tulkin, Steven R. "Race, Class, Family and School Achievement." *Journal of Personal and Social Psychology*, 9 (1968), 31–37.

The Structure of the American Public School

SCHOOLS AS CLOSED SYSTEMS

Chapters 2 through 5 have considered the reciprocal relationships between schools and the other institutions of society. In this chapter the focus narrows from consideration of the expectations of American society for its public schools to the subset of the American public school itself. There are thousands of members of that subset, thousands of schools in as many communities. A school is here defined as a complete social system usually within one building, and with one administrative leader, the principal. For clarity's sake, this chapter will generalize about the usual forms of school. If you find yourself taking exception to these generalizations in light of the schools best known to you, try to use the transformational model to clarify the differences you perceive and the possible reasons for them.

What strikes sociologists as both unusual and peculiarly characteristic of American schools is that they have tended to be closed systems. Most school systems act to restrict contact with the public they are meant to serve. A field trip into the community or a speaker from outside is the exception, not the rule. One rationale suggested for this is that the professional expertise of teachers is freer to operate without interference from a less knowledgeable community. (Eugene Litwak and Henry Meyer, 1974) This chapter will be very much concerned with the peculiarity of school closure to society. It is a "peculiarity" because no organic system can be completely closed: it takes effort to keep the barriers up. Nor has the American school system succeeded in becoming completely removed from the total system of American society in which it is situated. It is charged with responding to all the expectations described in Chapters 2 through 5. But as a rule, individual school units are closed off. American adolescents, you will discover, have found a way to keep that contact, even as they move about in their own high school. Critics of American schools in the last twenty years say that schools must change both in structure and function to catch up with their students in becoming more closely tied to modern life.

Why Schools Became Closed Off

A unique interaction between the particular characteristics of bureaucracy and the philosophical assumptions of capitalism may account for why schools have become closed systems. In Chapter 2, concerning government and decision making, the American school was described as typically bureaucratic. The characteristics of bureaucracy that were emphasized included:

1. Closely defined work rules
2. Specialized skills
3. Strictly prescribed roles

Historically, much formal education has taken place under other forms of social relations. Nobody rang any bells in ancient Athens; medieval monks might teach both viniculture and manuscript illumination; colonial teachers also brought in the coal and cleaned the outhouses.

Not all sociologists agree with Michael Katz's view (previously cited) that the bureaucratic pattern was universally adopted so the rising capitalist class of the mid-1800s might maintain control over the lower economic classes. Most believe, however, that bureaucracy in school was the natural result of schools seeking to conform to the society by which they had been created and into which their graduates moved.

Bureaucratic organization is common in other industrialized countries. It is found even in China and the Soviet Union despite their professed communist philosophy. American bureaucracy, however, is united with the economic philosophy of capitalism, which is based on a set of interlocking assumptions:

1. That all resources are scarce, while the demand for them is limitless
2. That the greatest good to the greatest number of persons occurs if men are free to compete unrestrictedly for command of those resources
3. That, as a result of this competition, social conflict is both expected and ultimately productive

Donald McKinley has shown how this ethos grew out of the earliest ideas of the Puritans and has been enlarged until it permeates our thoughts about American society and its schools. (McKinley, 1971) The American school developed its unique characteristics in response to this philosophy, as well as to the restrictions of bureaucratic organization.

The separation of the school from its community surroundings is an outgrowth of capitalistic bureaucracy. In order to economically manage the resources received from the rest of society, the school organization closed itself off. Especially when the community becomes aroused over the way the school is using tax resources, teachers and administrators defend themselves by claiming their professionalism gives them special expertise. They thus separate themselves from the "lay" community they serve. But while basing their claim to isolation on grounds of efficiency and expertise (main tenets of capitalism and bureaucracy), schools simultaneously run counter to the free enterprise philosophy because the clients (students) are forced to attend and have the service thrust upon them like prisoners. If the doors to other ways of spending time were open, how many student-clients would freely remain?

According to the capitalist theory, the economic marketplace establishes by supply and demand what enterprises shall survive, what inefficient ones wither away. But there is negligible

competition for the public schools. Only the rich have a choice
in the school market. Demands that schools become accountable, as are competing businesses, can create turmoil in the
educational community. School people usually claim that non-
school persons cannot judge the efficiency of their production,
and therefore educators can be accountable only to other educators, not "outsiders."

Parsons' model of social organization, our Figure 1.2, has
been used by traditionalist-minded educators to justify a system that operates on assumptions of industrial production and
system closure. If differences between the internal and external
exist, you can expect conflict at the barrier. Therefore it is best
to close off the barriers and discourage interaction (such as a
parent dropping in to visit the class unannounced). And if ends
and means are truly separate, then it is logical to plan for ends
(citizenship education, for example) and disregard the means
to that end (decision-making in this example).

What Is Wrong with a Closed System?

Although, as we saw in Chapter 2, in their first one hundred
years most American public schools adopted the bureaucratic
method of operation, today more and more educators are beginning to believe that the assumptions made by capitalism, bureaucracy, and the Parsons' model simply do not fit the school
system well, as had been previously thought. We have assumed
competition and conflict; we have assumed standardization
and interchangeable parts; we have assumed impermeable barriers and a separation of means and ends. Operating on these
assumptions, schools have striven to utilize bureaucratic procedures. Now questions regarding the utility of the bureaucratic
model for either analysis or school procedure are arising across
a wide spectrum of educational thinking. John Pincus, for example, accepts the concept that "the self-perpetuating bureaucracy of . . . public school governance is highly decentralized,"
but adds, "yet subject to a wide variety of influences so that
each unit perceives itself as facing a unique configuration of
clients and masters." (Pincus, 1974, p. 115)

John Walton, responding to the needs of future citizens, sees
a paradox:

> The conduct of education although dependent on bureaucratic organization, cannot be successfully bureaucratized. . . . For example, efficiency which is of the greatest value in purely organizational matters must allow for spontaneity, change, freedom, irregularity and the unexpected in teaching and learning. (Walton, 1974, p. 109)

Jean Dresden Grambs points out that personnel in the school system are continually making new decisions about unique events (people); that the school is staffed by persons with the same job title (teacher) but with greatly varying ability to develop a product which is never standard (learning); and that there is a very unclear division between policy and implementation. (Grambs, 1965) In other words, the way the American public school is structured bureaucratically and the conceptual tools previously used for analyzing it (the industrial model) are clearly not fitted to the nature of the educative process as we now understand it.

Meanwhile, students of American society influenced by books as diverse as economist John Kenneth Galbraith's *The New Industrial State* and modern mythmaker Charles Reich's *The Greening of America* are beginning to question whether pure capitalism is a valid picture of our present economic system. The postindustrial society may call for a new set of social and personal values other than those bureaucratic values now assumed in school and society. (John Platt, 1975) Organisms must grow and change to meet new challenges in their environment. But before we investigate these pressures for change on the organism of the school, we must examine more closely how public schools now operate and what specific problems this causes.

HOW TRADITIONAL SCHOOLS FUNCTION

Decision Making

In Chapter 2 some of the external political forces making decisions for the school were reviewed. Within the school itself are other decision makers, primarily the principal.

The principal's role is unique because it carries power. That is, what a principal decides should happen can be made to happen. One source of power is greater access to information. Grambs suggests that the principal's power is unrealistic because in many cases the teachers whom he or she directs actually know more. But while this may be true about the decisions to be made in individual classrooms about curriculum and learning, it does not hold in decisions about allocating resources—how many children a teacher shall be assigned, or what money should be spent for field trips versus outside speakers. Most important of all, the principal has the power to make decisions stick. He or she has access across the closed barrier of the school to the powerful support of parents and larger community through membership in local groups and attendance at the superintendent's cabinet meetings. System-management decisions that can affect teachers are the principal's responsibility, although he or she may indeed know less about various methods of teaching than does the newest teacher recruit.

The teachers have their own fields of decision making—their classrooms. Most of them guard their "autonomy" behind the closed door of the individual room, because there they can do as they think best in directing the learning of the pupils. Without an infusion of personal enthusiasm, they can cause a new instructional program to fail despite the principal's wishes. Today, through unionizing, teachers band together to take into their own hands more decision-making power in regard to system control (e.g., hours of work). At the same time, through a demand for teacher accountability, the educational hierarchy and the community aim to measure a teacher's power to make correct educational decisions.

Do the attendance-required clients, that is, the students, have any voice in decision making? This question will be explored further in Chapter 7, where we also investigate the classroom social system. In terms of the schoolwide impact of pupil decision making, however, their force is negative. That is, pupils can decide what *won't* happen more easily than they can determine what *will*. Teachers, for example, will reject any curriculum change out of hand if they suspect that students won't like the change, though they would be very reluctant indeed to implement a student-suggested change.

Allocation of Roles

In 1963 Jacob Getzels analyzed the cause of many disruptions found in schools as conflicts in role behavior on the part of teachers and pupils. (Getzels, 1963) All role behavior is a result of two kinds of needs seeking satisfaction simultaneously. Those needs that Getzels calls the *nomothetic* arise from the goals that society establishes to accomplish what "ought" or is expected to be. The human role player, with his or her idiosyncrasies arising from individual personal needs, contributes the *idiographic* dimension of role behavior. Conflict arises when these needs collide, for example when someone in the role of student must play "cut up."

Getzels also pointed out that conflicts may arise solely within the nomothetic dimension; for example, that between cultural values and institutional expectations, as in the "poor fit" of the bureaucratic model to schools. In the idiographic dimension a source of conflict may lie in the personality disposition of individuals and the several roles they must fill.

William Waller, who in 1933 wrote one of the earliest books on the sociology of education made a point of specifying the variety of roles that teachers are expected to play. This theme has been touched on by almost all subsequent writers on the profession of teaching.

As Getzels' word "idiographic" emphasizes, the personality of the individual teacher affects what role he or she plays most frequently—the model of community morality, the older friend, the stern taskmaster, or some other part. The age of the teacher may affect choice of role. This is due in part to cultural changes in society between the time when older and younger teachers were socialized. Further, one's views of what constitutes the teaching role may change with age and experience.

In addition to individual idiosyncrasies, role selection varies with the society in which a teacher works. The small rural community may expect a teacher to be a model of accepted behavior on and off the job. How late your car is parked in front of someone's home may be discussed all over town. Similarities or dissimilarities of ethnic background may structure the ability of a teacher to play the role of friend or older sibling.

The numerous variations that can arise when individuals take on these roles makes defining the characteristics of "good teaching" or a "good teacher" infinitely complex. What is right in one situation may in another role be behavior that will turn students away. Many adjustments would be called for if all elementary and secondary teachers switched job placements tomorrow.

If we narrowly define "good teachers" as those whose classes exceed the level of achievement predicted for them on present standardized tests, then two qualities share importance. Good teachers have high verbal ability, and they can convey to pupils an expectation for high achievement. (Wayne Gordon and Leta Adler, 1963)

Students, too, play roles, which will be discussed in Chapter 7. Other roles allocated in schools in addition to those of the teachers and administrators include various support personnel. School nurses frequently play other roles as psychological-counselor or family visitor. They may know more about the pupils than do the teachers. Some share this information; others withhold it, thereby gaining a certain power over their fellow professionals.

If you have not read Bel Kaufman's *Up the Down Staircase* (1964), do so soon. Ms. Kaufman's slightly fictionalized version of her own early years of teaching will make abundantly clear to you that those adults who do the major job of integrating and socializing in our schools today may be the custodians and the cafeteria workers. As in Ms. Kaufman's book, their influence is frequently beneficial—but there is neither guarantee nor check that this is so. Once again, the hidden curriculum is at work.

Integration

The society of the American public school is made up of adults who voluntarily offer a service and children who are required to be exposed to that offer. Traditionally, then, the power to integrate members and deliver sanctions has varied between the two groups. Teachers have had almost unlimited power over delivering sanctions to children. Children could respond with only the most subtle and devious sanctions against teachers because the teacher's legitimized power to punish might quickly come down upon their heads (or backs).

Functions that integrate teachers into the school continue to be reflected in certification requirements, which place barriers between the school and the job seeker. Those who meet these membership requirements are admitted; those who do not cannot teach in accredited schools. Once within the school, after a probationary period usually lasting three years, teachers are able to cement their membership in the school society by obtaining tenure, which means they cannot be let go except under the most extreme circumstances (usually involving moral turpitude). Tenured status has been looked upon as particularly important in American public schools where the whims of a political board of education might regard school jobs as just another form of patronage to be portioned out by the "ins."

Uniform attendance laws, meanwhile, mean that students have to come to school until well into their teens. Absence from school may land a young person in a detention home, by way of an "uncontrolled juvenile" decision by a judge. An aura of rigid conformity has made the climate of many schools more like jails than hospitals—two social institutions that also offer services to clients.

James Coleman, the author of the previously mentioned monumental study, *Equal Educational Opportunity*, is also well known for an earlier publication, *The Adolescent Society* (1961). In this volume, Coleman identifies a society of teen-agers making up a subculture within the school. This group is independent of the adult group, which occupies the same high-school building. The goals of the youths' subculture are not those of the teachers. Coleman's survey indicated that athletic prowess and popularity are more important goals for the youth, while the adult teachers, naturally enough, have goals of academic excellence. Other group tasks in addition to goal setting are also carried out by the members of the adolescent society, while the official school society simultaneously provides parallel functions.

In order to be with the society of their fellow teen-agers, many youth come to schools motivated quite independently of the required attendance law. So long as they attain success in the areas important to them, they meet the minimum requirements of the adults. To fail to meet adult standards brings sanctions that may drive them from both societies. Students voluntarily drop out only when they can play a role in neither the adult nor the adolescent society.

Socialization

Within the double society of the school, Coleman finds the task dimension as most important to adults. The students find greater significance in the membership dimension. Coleman's solution to the built-in competition between these two sets of norms is more competition in the form of academic games.

Critics of Coleman's study suggest that once again it is conditions in the larger society pushing upon the school that causes this apparent separation between the norms of the pupils and those of the teachers. The values of athletic prowess and popularity are the values of the adults outside the school—the parents, neighbors, and, indeed (if the truth be known) the teachers themselves when they are at home. By selecting only one dimension of human development for emphasis, the academic, the school has short-changed young people who are growing into a vastly wider world than the traditional school acknowledges. The young are simply imitating the elders in the society they will inherit, bypassing the culturally lagging adult society in the school. Students thus provide themselves with a more realistic acculturation than most schools provide.

THE SCHOOL IN DYNAMIC TRANSFORMATION: POSSIBLE ALTERNATIVES

The last two decades have seen a surge in school reform similar to the progressive school movement of the first part of our century. This section focuses on changes in overall school structure, with the advanced warning that the most significant movement for change may be occurring in individual classrooms rather than in the larger system of the school. These latter changes will be discussed in Chapter 7.

Using the transformational model, our consideration of these changes will focus on the interfaces between school and community, the grouping within school systems, the emphasis upon the individual or the group, and the task or membership dimension of education.

Opening the School System

Not surprisingly, efforts to bridge the gap between the community and the school were among the first changes made, and are most widely found. The movement for *community schools* began in the 1920s as a part of John Dewey's vision of relating school and society. Not only were students to seek curricula within the community, but the community was to be invited into the school for adult programs and to bring community members' expertise to bear on specific topics. In the United States, the most community schools are found in ghetto areas and have been suggested as an educational alternative on American Indian reservations. (*Alternative Schooling*, 1972) Their occurrence in these locations suggests that when schools fail most markedly, they ultimately turn to the community at their doors.

A particular experiment in community schools was the "schools without walls" program initiated by the Canadian John Bremer for the Philadelphia school system. Here, 134 students (chosen in order to guarantee they would randomly represent the socio-ethnic mix of center city) were encouraged to establish their own school. They were to utilize the social and cultural resources along the Benjamin Franklin Parkway in Philadelphia. These include various museums, institutes, and businesses. Classrooms, teachers, and material were the responsibility of the high-school youth to discover for themselves—an important reversal in role allocation in terms of decision making. The School District of Philadelphia acknowledged in a descriptive pamphlet that this program was set up particularly because schools are so closed off from society that pupils cannot learn how communities operate. (*Parkway Program*, 1971)

Two years after the publication of this pamphlet, the Philadelphia School Board refused to continue funding the Parkway Program. They acknowledged that it had an outstanding success, particularly with those youth who might have been dropouts. Part of the conflict that precipitated this decision was competition over who might have this high-demand resource. The new program couldn't expand fast enough for all students who wanted to participate.

In Chicago a similar program was established called the Metro school. Conflict arose when the program was being set up:

> The idea that really caught the eye of the school system's leadership was the school without walls concept. The central administration wanted a program that drew on community resources, but did not question the established educational patterns of the system—the way students relate to teachers, who makes decisions, and who controls the money. In contrast, Metro's consultants, teachers and students felt that the school without walls idea was meaningless unless it was coupled with an effort to achieve the school's other stated goals for humanizing education. (Robert Riorden, 1972, p. 33)

Metro's teachers were able to incorporate opportunities for student decision making and improved interpersonal relationships. (*Alternative Schooling*, 1972) They faced, however, with the Parkway school, the stress of being an *alternate school*—a school differing from the common pattern but under the jurisdiction of an established system. They confronted opposition:

> Several of the school system's central administrators reacted with positive hostility when it became apparent that Metro's program was challenging some of the cherished procedures of the school system. A second large group of central administrators was merely indifferent to Metro. Thus Metro's requests for equipment, assignment of staff, payment for outside services, and so on were treated with characteristic inefficiency, arbitrariness, and delay. The school system should have acknowledged the necessary connection between educational program change and change in administrative procedures. Such a relationship was not accepted, however. (Riorden, 1972, p. 36)

Alternate schools within established districts that have seemed to flourish are those that preach the back-to-basics philosophy, whose structure and function most closely resemble the schools of the nineteenth and early twentieth centuries. ("Back to Basics," 1974) Springing from a source common to today's usual school structures, these schools perhaps put less strain on the system, while permitting parents and teachers somewhat of a choice in the method of education.

Regrouping Students

Other structural changes that schools within public systems have introduced are mini-schools that regroup students from within one unit to smaller subsystems. The goal here is to increase the sense of understanding and identity between staff and pupils.

Structural changes in time occur when "problem students" —for example, potential dropouts, underachievers—are pulled out of the regular stream, given a period of intense individual attention or a different curricula, and then returned to regular classes hopefully "cured" of their school sickness. ("Alternative Educational Programs," 1974)

Significantly, there is almost no data to show that varying class size or grouping students differently than the traditional age-segregated classrooms makes a difference in pupil achievement. Social scientists have long expected to find significant results by varying class size and age composition, but no evidence has been properly replicated so far.

Emphasizing the Individual

There is considerable confusion between two terms that describe schools in which the individual is emphasized to a greater degree than is a class grouping. *Open schools* are based on a structured theory of learning that uses a coordinated series of stimulating settings to maximize a child's learning potential. Such a school may operate in an established public system, in one room of such a system, or as a private venture operating independently of the public schools. Changes in roles and structure that this basic change in purpose suggests will be discussed in greater detail in the next chapter.

Free schools, since their idiosyncratic characteristics all but guarantee they cannot be contained within a public school, are frequently categorized with any school operating outside the established system. More properly, however, free schools are

those that have no institutionalized expectations, either for behavior or curriculum. Traditional curriculum is de-emphasized
because it *is* traditional. Teachers are central to the format of
free schools since their individual abilities and character determine what the children shall learn. The idiographic dimension
of the teaching role is therefore paramount. Because individual
freedom is paramount, free schools have few structural supports. Their average life span has been just nine months.

Free schools and open schools have been among the most
widespread reforms in the last decade. But notice that their
shared emphasis upon the individual also occurs when the
reforms discussed in previous sections are adopted. Indeed,
Douglas Watson claims that the most common thrust of alternative schools is toward increased individualization of student programs. (Watson, 1972)

Emphasizing Membership

A movement away from the task-oriented school toward one
that stresses the importance of the emotional component of
human living is described in *The Human Relations School* by
Robert Fox and Ronald Lippitt. (Fox and Lippitt, 1968) Although the school model depicted does not exist, the proposed
changes readily fit our transformational model. Cooperation
supplants competition as barriers between coworkers are permeated. A wider variety of human resources and community
involvement occurs when the school and community are open
to each other. Continuing in-service training for teachers and
continuous evaluative feedback reflect a view of the school as a
growing organism, rather than a once-given static structure,
changeless through time.

Another effort to meet the problems of today with an emphasis upon the membership dimension was tried in 1969 when a
group of children from several racial backgrounds were
brought together to improve their understanding of other persons. Aesthetic experiences were used as the content for this
process of increased understanding, as the title of the children's own report suggests—"Yesterday I Learned There Was
Forever." (*Alternative Schooling*, 1972, p. 9)

As we shall see in the next chapter, at the elementary level the British have leaped ahead of Americans in developing the open classroom model of learning. A comparable forward leap has been made by the British at the high-school level. A group of dropouts developed a summer-school curriculum for themselves that adequately reflected what they needed to know to enter modern British society in their early teens. (*Alternative Schooling*, 1972, p. 10) The materials developed by these young people from the song lyrics and newspaper photographs of the 1960s and 1970s are of excellent quality. One can only wonder at the slowness of both British and American schools in adopting this student-made curriculum (or one like it) for those who plunge into the realities of daily breadwinning early. Indeed, all the youth who must someday "cope" might benefit from a similar self-developed curriculum.

Apparently one of the factors that freed these British youth to make significant and creative curriculum was a change in their roles and relationships with teachers. Teachers began to treat these adolescents with the respect they paid other adults. Significantly, the curriculum these youth developed was high in the affective or feeling component. They sensed that "learning to relate," the membership dimension of their group existence, was of high priority as they moved toward tomorrow.

An Evaluation of Actual Change

The Educational Clearinghouse data from *Alternative Schooling* (1972) that we have been citing above provided us with a very small number of instances of change in the public-school system. How much change has actually occurred in the last ten years?

Six years after their strong 1968 criticism of the American public schools entitled *Teaching as a Subversive Activity*, Neil Postman and Charles Weingartner had come to believe "large numbers of school people ... have heard the hollering and have made some effort to modify the schooling process." (Postman and Weingartner, 1974, p. 17) They make a distinction, however, between the essential functions of the school (such as structuring time and evaluating children), which have remained relatively unchanged, and the unconventional ways some schools are fulfilling these functions. As an example of the latter, they cite some schools that provide varying modules of time for different learning tasks and thus move away from "factory-like processing procedures and toward more humanistic, individualized judgments." (p. 35) Postman and Weingartner believe the direction of change in schools today is precisely in such "good" directions as these.

A National Consortium of Alternative Schools was set up at Indiana University in 1972 in order to set up alternate school forms within a single public-school system.

Douglas Watson, in his book *Alternative Schools* (1972), noted that while facilities costs may be low since many alternate schools dispense with such "frills" as lunchrooms and gyms, other costs are higher in highly individualized, low student/teacher ratio programs. Acknowledging the difficulties such schools seem to encounter, Watson offered varied advice to those who would establish such alternatives. Significantly, perhaps, all his suggestions represented retreats to the traditional when conflict arose.

Still, as Watson notes, alternate schools in public systems, like the voucher plan, have some intrinsic value: "The idea of providing alternative learning options is based on an entirely different conception of change. For rather than pushing people around you provide options that attract people to them. They choose. They make decisions." (Watson, quoting Mario Fantini, 1972, p. 3)

One positive advantage of alternate schools, even when they fail, is that they are able to inspire change in the rest of the system. This happened with the Parkway Program in Philadelphia, which resulted in the establishment of that city's Office of Alternative Programs.

Recently, no less prestigious an institution than Teachers College of Columbia University sent out a call for papers dealing with implementing change in schools. It intends to devote a special 1976 issue of the *Teachers College Record* to this topic because:

> Most educators realize that the amount and pace of change has fallen far short of initial expectations. The problem is more profound than simply pointing at the unrealistic impatience of the Sixties. Programs were planned, curriculum was developed,

teaching/learning units were packaged, teachers were trained, and the results were frustrating, uneven, unexpected, and temporary. With hindsight it is easy to see that designing and disseminating change is not implementing change. What happens inside the school at the service delivery level is absolutely crucial to our success or failure, yet the gap in our knowledge about implementing change in the school is formidable. ("Special Issue of *Teachers College Record*," 1975, p. 24)

To say the gap is formidable is not to say it cannot be bridged. Indeed, publications like the one described are one way to cope with our present ignorance. So long as many educators believe change is necessary and wish to change, what better basis for believing it possible?

MAIN IDEAS

1. The structure of the American school system derives particularly from its previous interaction with a bureaucratic-capitalistic society.
2. Competition and conflict have characterized the American school as well as American society. The school system is closed from the community as a result of the behavior arising from the assumptions that regulate a bureaucratic-capitalistic society. Problems of several sorts may result because of the intrinsic inability of education to thrive given these assumptions.
3. Decision making in the present system is generally in the hands of principals and teachers, with pupils exercising a limited negative power.
4. Teachers may play a variety of roles in their relation to students, as do various support personnel.
5. Integration of the school society is generally achieved by legal sanctions against truancy for children and bureaucratic regulation for adults.
6. The adolescent society does not share the same ordering of norms as their teachers but more closely resembles the values of the larger culture.

7. Possible alternate models of schools have been concerned with breaking down school-community barriers, grouping students in nontraditional ways, emphasizing individual rather than group goals, and upgrading the socio-emotional rather than task dimension of school life.

8. In spite of multiple efforts to change and reform schools, little evidence exists that to date change has seriously affected educational outcomes, though educators are more aware now of the need for real change.

GLOSSARY

alternate schools   Those schools that differ from the common pattern of established schools, but may exist as an option within a given public system.

community schools   Schools that allow students to seek learning in their local communities and encourage community members to participate in the schools.

free schools   Those schools that emphasize the idiosyncrasies of the teacher and the immediate moment, in sharp contrast to the bureaucratic expectations of most other schools.

idiographic dimension   The individual, personal need dimension of social behavior.

nomothetic dimension   The normative (normal) or socially expected dimension of social behavior.

open schools   Those schools that emphasize a structured sequence of stimulating experience to maximize individual learning.

SUGGESTED ACTIVITIES

1. Arrange to discuss the concept of teacher accountability with persons who may hold different views: a school board member, a classroom teacher, an officer in a teachers' union or association, and/or several taxpayers.

2. Prepare (and deliver if you can) a series of role-playing situations that illustrate Getzels' analysis as described in this chapter. You may wish to read the original article, which is listed in the bibliography, in order to better appreciate the concept.

3. Prepare a critique of James Coleman's *The Adolescent Society* in terms of the teen culture that existed in your own high school. How did your experience illustrate or contradict Coleman's hypotheses?

4. Has a school district in your area established an alternate school? The principal or parent involved in founding it might be able to give you information regarding its reasons for being started, problems encountered, and its successes and failures to date.

5. Investigate preschool and continuing education programs as enlarged transactions between schools and society. Newspaper files may reveal what forces supported their establishment in your community.

6. What changes in the role of the school are seen by the principal, teachers, and community workers of a community school available for your study?

7. Read and compare Neil Postman and Charles Weingartner's *Teaching as a Subversive Activity* with their later publication *How to Recognize a Good School* (see bibliography). Does the second volume adequately respond to the criticisms in the first?

BIBLIOGRAPHY

"Alternative Educational Programs: Promise or Problems." *Educational Leadership*, XXXII, 2 (November 1974), 83–127.

Alternative Schooling: New Patterns in Education, No. 22 of the ERIC abstracts published by the American Association of School Administrators. Eugene: ERIC Clearinghouse on Educational Management, University of Oregon, 1972.

"Back to Basics." *Newsweek*, 21 October 1974, p. 95.

Coleman, James. *The Adolescent Society*. New York: Free Press, 1961.

Fox, Robert S., and Ronald Lippitt. *The Human Relations School.* Ann Arbor: Center for Research on Utilization of Scientific Knowledge, University of Michigan, 1968.

Galbraith, John Kenneth. *The New Industrial State.* Boston: Houghton Mifflin, 1967.

Getzels, Jacob W. "Conflict and Role Behavior in the Educational Setting." In *Readings in the Social Psychology of Education.* Ed. W. W. Charters, Jr., and N. L. Gage. Boston: Allyn & Bacon, 1963, pp. 309–18.

Giacquinta, Joseph B. "The Process of Organization Change in Schools." In *Review of Research in Education.* Ed. Fred N. Kerlinger. Itasca, Ill.: F. E. Peacock, 1973. I, 178–208.

Glaser, Robert. "Individuals and Learning: The New Aptitudes." *Educational Researcher,* June 1972, pp. 5–13.

Gordon, C. Wayne, and Leta M. Adler. *Dimensions of Teacher Leadership in Classroom Social Systems.* Los Angeles: University of California, Department of Education, 1963. Mimeographed report.

Grambs, Jean Dresden. *Schools, Scholars, and Society.* Englewood Cliffs, N.J.: Prentice-Hall, 1965.

Katz, Michael B. *Class, Bureaucracy, and Schools, The Illusion of Educational Change in America.* New York: Praeger, 1971.

Kaufman, Bel. *Up the Down Staircase.* Englewood Cliffs, N.J.: Prentice-Hall, 1964.

Litwak, Eugene, and Henry J. Meyer. *School, Family and Neighborhood, The Theory and Practice of School-Community Relations.* New York: Columbia University Press, 1974.

McKinley, Donald G. "The Ethos of Industrial America." In *Society and Education: A Book of Readings,* 2nd ed. Ed. Robert G. Havighurst et al. Boston: Allyn & Bacon, 1971, pp. 2–11.

Parkway Program. Philadelphia: School District of Philadelphia, 1971.

Pincus, John. "Incentives for Innovation in the Public Schools." *Review of Educational Research,* XLIV, 1 (Winter 1974), 113–44.

Platt, John. Address before Second General Assembly of the World Futures Society. Washington, D.C., 3 June 1975.

Postman, Neil, and Charles Weingartner. *How to Recognize a Good School.* Bloomington, Ind.: Phi Delta Kappan Educational Foundation, 1974.

————. *Teaching as a Subversive Activity.* New York: Delta Books, 1969.

Reich, Charles A. *The Greening of America.* New York: Random House, 1970.

Riorden, Robert C. *Alternate Schools in Action.* Bloomington, Ind.: Phi Delta Kappan Educational Foundation, 1972.

"Special Issue of *Teachers College Record* on 'Implementing Change in

Schools,' " *The Generator* of Division G, American Educational Research Association, V, 2 (Winter 1975), 24.

Walton, John. "The Study of Education: Prisoner of Metaphor and Synecdoche." *Educational Studies*, V, 3 (1974), 103–10.

Watson, Douglas. *Alternative Schools: Pioneering Districts Create Options for Students.* Arlington, Va. : National School of Public Relations Association, 1972.

The Social System of the Classroom

THE CLASSROOM AND THE SCHOOL SYSTEM

In this chapter our attention shifts to the classroom, defined as a group of children, selected by some rationale (usually age), and an instructing adult who are brought together in order to accomplish a task assigned by the larger society, school, and community of which they are a part. What is the classroom's relation to the school? According to one author:

> The classroom is a subsystem of the school, a dependent part of the whole. Decisions made by administrators of an organization determine the method and content of classroom instruction, the size of the class, the goals of the organization, the characteristics of the classroom teachers, the hierarchy of personnel, the stratification of the students, and the degree of school-community interaction. (Patricia Sexton, 1967, p. 65)

If this view is correct, then the classroom, as the creature of the larger school system, is completely dependent on that system's making the first move if reform is desired. In fact, the same author goes on to say, "Decisions made at the top can even abolish the classroom and establish alternative patterns of organization such as an independent or group study, tutorials, or mass media instruction, none of which needs a traditional classroom." (Sexton, p. 65)

Many educational reformers favor abolition of the traditional classroom—that long-standing educational institution that continues to be the primary unit where "teaching" and "learning" are supposed to occur. But if they share with Sexton the view of the classroom as the passive tool of the system, their hope for reform is doomed. As Chapter 6 has stressed, decisions made at the top rarely succeed—and bureaucracies rarely make decisions to change. We hold, instead, that if the school system is to be transformed, the changes may have to begin at the classroom level. In the rest of the chapter, after clarifying ideas on how the traditional classroom works, we will focus on the kinds of grassroots reforms that are taking place in the classroom today.

HOW TRADITIONAL CLASSROOMS FUNCTION

Decision Making

One of the most characteristic aspects of a traditional class is the concentration of the power over decision making, and all other group tasks, in the hands of one member—the teacher. The ascribed role exists because of achievement outside of the immediate group situation. In the room the teacher's status is presumed to be primary. Because of the teacher's previous achievement, society has awarded her or him the job. Children will test a teacher's power to see if it is real. When decisions are made to come about, however, the students generally quickly acquiesce to their inferior position on the decision-making ladder. This is the reason new teachers are admonished never to make a threat or promise of punishment unless they intend to carry it out. At the same time, they must be careful to follow through on promised activities or rewards. When students perceive that the high-status person either will not or cannot follow through on his or her decisions, they perceive that person as powerless. What results is chaos.

Chaos results because, in spite of the subtle presence of student groups such as the adolescent society, there is no readily available other system of decision making about instructional tasks. Task decisions are available only to teachers.

At the same time, students do have some degree of power when the membership, not the task, dimension is considered. Observers can usually pick out the class leaders as well as the class scapegoat—the one with no friends and to whom no one defers. There is a pecking order among classmates. Friendship choices among students are an integral part of this system.

Sociograms are a method of diagraming the choices persons make of those other group members with whom they would like to work or play. First employed in the 1930s by T. L. Moreno, sociograms have been used frequently by sociological researchers and by many classroom teachers. The analysis begins by asking individual class members one or more questions about others with whom they would like to work or play.

How the question is posed directly influences the choices persons make. For example, is the situation to be task- or membership-oriented? Sociograms measure group cohesiveness on just one variable at just one time. In any situation, however, sociograms show "stars" who are chosen by many members of the group and "isolates" who may be chosen by no one. Social attraction thus gives power to a few in the class. Since stars frequently choose each other, powerful coalitions may be formed. Most group members are chosen by a few and choose a few others, and a very small number remain outside the group chosen by no one.

Sociograms apparently are a good measure of group members' satisfaction. One might expect greater satisfaction to lead to higher student performance. Except in the case of successful attempts to involve isolates, however, a recent review of the literature indicates "good group relations make no contribution to academic performance goals and may in fact work against such goals if the group is unified in its nonacceptance of achievement values." (Sarane S. Boocock, 1972, p. 169) If, on the other hand, the student's peer group values school achievement, he or she will be more likely to achieve. For example, one study of Catholic Americans concluded: "Not only do Catholic schools accelerate the upward mobility of Catholics, but they apparently do so through some kind of complicated operation of friendship patterns among young Catholics." (Andrew Greeley and Peter Rossi, 1966, p. 225)

Evidence exists that teachers actively cooperate with the students' social system. They apparently permit students to have the power of making membership decisions to avoid conflict or competition in decisions regarding task completion. (Elizabeth Cohen, 1972) Further, in one researcher's flat summation of the role of peer values, "educational programs that work against important peer values are doomed to failure." (Boocock, 1972, p. 240)

In addition to status based on social power and related bonds of attraction, student status is also affected by race, age, and sex just as it is in society in general. Further, in the academic atmosphere of the school, position on the achievement scale is also important. Children's status in the classroom determines their approach to the assigned task, and the teacher's reaction to them. Teachers respond differently to children, depending on their respective positions on the ruler of achievement. (Cohen, 1972) On the other hand, research has found that lower social-class children were placed in the back of kindergarten rooms *regardless* of their reading-readiness scores. (R. Rist, 1970) As in all things dealing with the human animal, no simple conclusions are possible when assessing the status of a particular individual. We do know, however, that students' status directly affects their learning potential by determining decisions made about them by a teacher and their own decisions about whether or not they will work on the instructional task.

The task the teacher decides to pursue may fall along a broad range. At one end of this continuum the task may be conceived as the traditional one of transmitting those aspects of the past culture that society has decided have been needed by its new members. (One might refer to this position as the pâté de fois gras school of pedagogy: grab the student by the neck and jam the information down his intellectual throat as if you were force-feeding a goose. The student has no choice, nor perhaps does the teacher whose syllabus may be state-defined.) On the other end of the continuum is the conception of the teacher's task as encouragement of a student's maximum free development. In this classroom, the child is the center of the curriculum.

Following the Sputnik-induced panic of the 1960s, several professional organizations of physicists, chemists, and biologists attempted to construct "teacher-proof" curricula. These courses of study were so organized that students would be able to learn the subject matter in spite of, or despite, the vagaries of the individual instructor. A decade later, however, no differences were found between the achievement of students who had studied the same material with either the old or new teacher-proof curricula. (Decker Walker and Jon Schaffarzick, 1974) Apparently, as shall be discussed in greater detail below, the learning environment of the classroom is very much more complex than we have previously understood and is going to require much more sophisticated methods of study and prescription for change.

Allocation of Roles

Status differences between teacher and students, and among students, differentiate the roles they play as described above. Two other important sociological factors also influence the classroom system of role allocation.

One of these is the system of grouping students in a classroom. Almost all schools in the United States group the student body into classes on the basis of age. Because the human animal passes through identifiable developmental stages, age has always been a handy categorizing device. Grouping children by just one dimension (like age) is called *homogeneous grouping*. As has been known for centuries, but verified with the introduction of achievement tests, children at any age vary greatly in their ability to perform school tasks associated with that age. Some schools, therefore, further group the children on the basis of their IQ or reading score. Such grouping is the more commonly understood meaning of homogeneous grouping. Students may also be grouped homogeneously for reading instruction and then regrouped homogeneously on the basis of their mathematics achievement.

Heterogeneous grouping, on the other hand, more closely resembles the one-room schoolhouse. Here children of a wide range of school ability are found in the same instructional group. In the British family system of classroom organization, age may vary also.

The argument over which is the better method of allocating children to classes has been decided in a perhaps unexpected way. Students, except for those with very poor or very outstanding intellectual ability, generally do better in heterogeneous classes, regardless of their own level of competence. On the other hand, teachers feel it is much easier to teach homogeneous classes, and therefore schools continue to allocate students in this fashion.

Another important sociological factor in role allocation in the classroom is the increased utilization of students as teachers. Their services may be in the form of an "oral report," leadership of a subgroup studying a particular topic, or one-to-one tutoring by those who complete the assigned work first (the so-called Keller plan). The reasons for this trend surely include the residue of John Dewey's philosophy that we learn by doing. Another source is the psychology of Jean Piaget, which emphasizes the utilization of feedback from peers as the school-age child progresses in intellectual development. Further, the teacher, by careful selection of the student as teacher, may manipulate, maximizing or diminishing leadership patterns among the students.

Delivery of Sanctions

Our discussion of the task dimensions of the classroom so far has emphasized how integral they are with the membership dimensions. Questions of delivering sanctions and the utilization of discipline have already been discussed in relation to decision making and role allocation. Recent research suggests modifications in the teacher's traditional role of disciplinarian.

One of these modifications results from a discovery of the child's perception of punishment. Most school-age children apparently are more devoted to reciprocity than mercy. Laurence Kohlberg's studies of moral development suggest that preadolescents may literally be unable to grasp adult concepts of justice. (Kohlberg, 1971) The teacher may wish "to temper the wind to the shorn lamb," but "making the punishment fit the crime" will be seen as more fair by the pupils—for whom fairness is a primary value. Individual children, especially in junior and senior high school, may have attained an adult level of morality. As a result it is recommended that a teacher must take this individual factor into consideration, as well as many others, in dispensing punishment. The goal is for the child clearly to perceive the teacher's distaste for the transgression, but undergirding this is interest and concern for the pupil.

Another modification of teacher as disciplinarian stems from utilization in the last decade of the concepts of psychologist B. F. Skinner to maintain a favorable classroom atmosphere. As described in Chapter 4, this Harvard professor has fathered a method of modifying the behavior of individuals through a careful schedule of rewards or reinforcements. In his utopian novel, *Walden Two* (1962), punishment is banished and individual behavior is controlled by manipulation of the contingencies of the environment, ranging from food rewards to personal internalized social approval. Readers respond differently to this book. Some are revolted by what they see as a loss of personal freedom; others are so enthusiastic they have established communities similar to the one described in *Walden Two*. Several volumes exist that describe these methods of group integration, and you might want to consult them. Many teachers have found behavioral modification the answer to unruly classes.

If students (1) find the tasks assigned are meaningful to them, (2) get a sense of satisfaction from completing them, and (3) believe the teacher sees them as persons who can and will achieve, discipline (the delivery of sanctions) will be almost always unnecessary. Integration will take place because the teacher's goals have been adopted by the pupils as *their* goals, and when that move to individual enculturation takes place, the group task of formal and structured integration is no longer needed.

Some teachers, especially in the elementary school, utilize the socio-emotional aspect of human interaction to get classroom tasks done by overwhelming students. They pour out on their students quantities of love and affection. Classrooms become "love-ins." Patricia Lawler refers to this as "wallowing in sentimentality over the gardens of enchantment for little people." (Lawler, 1974, p. 64) As Lawler points out, the reality of our society and the typical high-school preparation for it make such an approach particularly inappropriate. Further, it stunts the child's ability to develop relationships with adults on a basis other than that of the socio-emotional. One socializing function of schools is to wean students from this family way of relating to the more formal task-oriented relationships existing outside the family.

Other teachers, in order to control classes, keep them so perpetually occupied with busy work that neither chaos nor learning takes place. (L. Smith and W. Geoffrey, 1968) Such classrooms may give the appearance of learning, as surely as many nineteenth-century classrooms did. Today, however, we have more sophisticated technology for helping learning to occur and more subtle methods of measuring the success of a variety of learning activities and goals.

Communication

With the development of computer technology, the word *communication* has been expanded to mean all informational processes that develop between two systems. That could be Mary speaking to her dog, the President addressing Congress, or a student interacting with a machine in computer-assisted instruction.

The type of group integration taking place is frequently reflected in the nature of the communications occurring. Figure 1.1 suggests the kinds of communication flow that can take place in a classroom.

If the goal is to purvey an agreed-upon curriculum of fact, the best method of communication is an uninterrupted one-way flow of information with the teacher at the front of the room in control of communication and the students facing forward. If the goal is to teach by the so-called discovery method, emphasizing the learning of a learning process perhaps, then communication must involve fellow learners. In a circular pattern, the teacher may act as a regulator on the group by providing feedback out of his or her store of knowledge. Perhaps this could be diagramed with the pupils in a circle, the teacher in the center—or wandering around from lab table to lab table as pupils discover on their own. If the goal is to change attitudes, or to teach the youth better ways to relate, the teacher might join the circle and take part as just one other member of the group—reserving his or her special talents to later interpret the dynamics of the group's interaction.

Because communication patterns thus suggest the nature of

the roles and goals of a group, as well as the integration of the members, many studies of classroom social structure have analyzed the flow of classroom communication. Ned A. Flanders' Categories of Interaction Analysis (1960) and R. F. Bales' Process Analysis (1950) are two descriptions of behavior that have been used widely. Forms of these descriptions are included under "Suggested Activities" at the end of this chapter.

Bales focused upon goal-directed behavior to analyze leadership communication. Flanders categorized classroom verbal interaction as being either teacher or student initiated.

In the numerous studies by many examiners who have utilized these analytic forms, two important facts have become clear. Communication cannot be viewed as a one-way process. Biosystems interact with their environment, barriers are permeable. For this reason, these interaction analyses show only half or less of the true picture. Students and teachers are also at the receiving ends of these communications, and they respond as individuals.

Also, human communication is dynamic; it takes place over time. Situations and communications that have preceded the moments considered in an analysis also affect what pattern will be revealed there. These previous interactions may themselves be both hidden and more significant.

Most recently, analyses that focus solely upon verbal communication (as does that of Flanders) have come under attack. Nonverbal messages of communication expressed in body language, the arched eyebrow, the sleeping student form, also reflect the interaction between the systems brought together in a group. (Robert and Anita Woolfolk, 1974; Charles Galloway, 1974)

Establishment of Norms

What causes an individual member of the class to accept the group goal of learning as his or her own goal? To move from extrinsic (caused by forces outside the individual) to intrinsic motivation? To become self-motivated to learn?

Almost the entire domain of the psychological foundations of education deals in one way or another with these questions of individual learning and motivation. It would be redundant and impractical to attempt a review of that system of concepts here. But, as sociologists, can we identify particular variables of enculturation that result from the individual's membership in various groups?

Chapter 5 reviewed all the subcultural components carried through an individual's family membership that affect his perception and acceptance of the student role. Historical studies (J. W. Atkinson, 1964) and anthropological studies (H. A. Barry et al., 1959) have suggested that economics also has a broad impact on motivation to learn. The influence of peer groups was reviewed above as well as in Chapter 5.

Sociologists may focus their study of education upon the action of humans as group members, looking at the total gestalt, the total pattern. Social psychologists remind us, however, that each part (each human being) is the result of a unique blend of hereditary factors that have interacted over at least six years, and perhaps many more, with an equally unique personal environment. In order to better understand and teach these individuals, we study hypotheses relating to their common or similar behavior in groups—but the basic unit is characteristic individuality. What motivates Sam is not what motivates Mary. No one else has ever been motivated in quite this way, nor will anyone ever be so motivated again. The teacher may have to review many possible variables affecting his or her pupils before discovering the key to enculturating each one into the learning group.

Praise is rather generally considered as reinforcing for most humans, causing them to continue to exhibit the desired behavior. But researchers have shown that even such a straightforward variable as a student's responsiveness to praise may be influenced by a previous record of failure, the difficulty of the task involved, and whether or not the child believes he or she has some real control over the particular environment. (Alfred Lintner and Joseph DuCette, 1974)

When one reviews the essential individuality of each person's needs and motivation, it is not surprising to find that the uniform educational treatment children get in most classrooms has failed to result in their maximum commitment to and benefit from learning. As Lintner and DuCette point out, the standard remark, "That was very good, class," will be responded to differently by the individual students, each of whom hears the same words.

Those teachers who prefer homogeneous classrooms may fail to realize that grouping by one dimension, such as age or reading ability, does not produce homogeneity of motivation or learning style. Thus one of the most constraining aspects of the status quo is the myth of homogeneous classrooms. An apparent sameness disguises more real differences.

THE CLASSROOM IN DYNAMIC TRANSFORMATION: REASONS FOR CHANGE

Change in the Notion of Aptitude

One new concept from the field of psychology points to change in the concept of grouping children by learning abilities. The traditional test of intelligence, the so-called intelligence quotient or IQ, related a child's achievement to his age. But it is rapidly being replaced by definitions of ability that are much more specific. Intelligence (or the ability to succeed in learning) is now seen as being composed of a variety of aptitudes.

Some aptitudes are cognitive, such as the ability to expand and elaborate upon a given concept. Some are affective, such as the ability to control impulsive action. An individual's school ability (intelligence) is composed of a unique pattern of aptitudes such as these, only some of which are believed presently to be identifiable. (Robert Glaser, 1972)

At the same time, work has already begun to fit learning tasks to the aptitudes already identified. This new concept is known as *aptitude-treatment interaction (ATI)*. If this more specific method of education were adopted, teaching would resemble a doctor's prescribing a certain treatment for a certain malady. Research has even shown that not only can a pupil's ability to use an aptitude be maximized, but we may actually *improve* that aspect of his intelligence. (W. D. Rohwer, 1971)

This view of learning is highly individualized. Pupils might still be grouped for common treatment if they shared a common level of a specific aptitude, but the refinement and specificity of the aptitude and treatment would suggest much smaller groups, meeting for much shorter periods of time than the traditional twenty to forty pupil classroom of forty to sixty minutes.

There is an additional benefit of this new allocation of student time and effort. We can counteract some of the overwhelming influence on learning behavior caused by students' status on a composite achievement ladder. "We can redesign the tasks in the classroom so that students display a broader range of talent to each other, thus destroying the 'single human ability' idea underlying the dysfunctional effects of status." (Cohen, 1972, p. 450) As suggested below, this will call for a shifting pattern of student roles.

Curriculum Change

ATI suggests a new view of the learner that emphasizes his or her nature as a unique system. At the same time, however, the traditional curriculum disciplines once thought of as discrete systems of knowledge are now beginning to blend. New realms of human discovery include social psychology, biochemistry, oceanography, urban problems. These new curriculum titles reflect the increasing emphasis of scholars upon the areas where information is best gained from combining a variety of the traditional disciplines.

Education itself is now beginning to see its relation not only to psychology and philosophy, from which it sprang as a study in the early twentieth century, but also to public policy (government), history, economics, international studies, administrative procedures and curriculum development, as well as the teaching and learning processes. This list comes from the table of contents of a journal of book reviews published by the American Educational Studies Association in 1974. The closed systems of traditional disciplines are opening for interactions with many other "courses of study."

Change of Aims

A third trend on which we will focus in even greater detail in the final chapter deals with a reconsideration of the aims of education. Historically, the tradition of cultural transmission has focused upon *what* is to be learned. The major impact of the progressive school movement of the early 1900s was to emphasize the *who* of the learner, the individual child. Encompassing both these, the future may call for education emphasizing the *how* of learning. Since we can only partially predict and control the future, we must transmit skills of learning that can be used to solve whatever novel problems arise.

As suggested at the end of the chapters dealing with the social environment of the schools, the transformation needed for the future is a new perspective on the teaching-learning process focusing upon:

1. Learning how to choose
2. Learning how to value
3. Learning how to learn
4. Learning how to relate to others

Learning activities that cannot be supported by reference to one of these four goals are probably entropic.

Change in the Roles of Instructor and Student

When the concepts of ATI, curriculum integration, and change in educational aims interact with one another, a change in role function is also required. Psychologist Carl Rogers expressed this idea dramatically in 1970 by recommending that educators "forget you were ever a teacher." Rather than teaching, Rogers called for adult classroom teachers to become facilitators of learning, and he spelled out what sort of change in role behavior this called for.

What we have called the pâté de fois gras school of pedagogy, Rogers calls "the mug and jug" theory.

> "How can I make the mug hold still while I fill it from the jug with these facts which I regard as so valuable?" The facilitator asks an entirely different question, primarily having to do with the climate. "How can I create a psychological climate in which the child will feel free to be curious, will feel free to make mistakes and learn from them, will feel free from judgmental evaluation, will feel free to learn from his environment, his fellow students, from me, and from his experience? How can I help him recapture the excitement of learning which was his in infancy?" (Rogers, 1970, p. 35)

Such a change in "teaching" role will naturally institute a change in student roles. Alvin Toffler, looking toward that future, described a variety of these transformations:

> Classes with several teachers and a single student; classes with several teachers and a group of students; students organized into temporary task forces and project teams; students shifting from group work to individual or independent work and back; all these and their permutations will need to be employed to give the student some advanced taste of the experience he will face later on . . . (Toffler, 1970, p. 409)

POSSIBLE ALTERNATE FORMS

The bureaucratic pattern of operation cannot accomodate the avenues of change suggested above where roles are shifting and constantly redefined, individuality rather than standardization determines ways and means, and rules and requirements are fluid (though no less real). Those school forms that adopt a nonbureaucratic model, that focus upon transmitting skills for today and tomorrow, are pointing the way toward the transformation of the schools.

One successful alternative form is called the open school; it has a tradition going back to the turn of the century. Other successful alternate forms employ the most modern technology, but in individualistic ways, allowing machinery to maximize possible choices of learning. A final form to consider is that which defies the assumption of the school as a closed system and attempts to bring the reality of the wider social system into the classroom.

The Open School

The most well known example of one model of an alternate form of education is in the open school, briefly discussed in the last chapter. Historically, the concept began with the American educator-philosopher John Dewey in the early 1900s. But Americans, with their cultural tradition of hurry-up and make-do, scuttled the potential of Dewey's ideas of progressive education with a too hasty application of what they did not understand

and were not trained to teach. Meanwhile, in England, the ideas of progressive education grew slowly, and with the 1967 publication of Lady Plowden's report on the British infants school, the "new" model of progressive education was again presented to the international educational community.

In the United States the idea of the open school received wide publicity in 1970 when Charles Silberman suggested it as a solution in his book *Crisis in the Classroom.* Silberman's book spread the idea that crises were endemic in the schools of the United States. Many volumes followed that described the open-school concept, but perhaps one of the best is Virgil Howes' *Informal Teaching in the Open Classroom.* His "Introduction" briefly describes what the open classroom is and what it is not:

> Resources are viewed not in terms of material things alone, but in terms of ideas emerging from children, experiences shared by classmates, and everyday things provided close at hand. And teachers, as humans, facilitate, guide and serve, thus replacing manipulation and domination. But love is not enough. The teacher acts in positive ways to help bring the child to consciousness that which he is experiencing, to link learnings, and to turn activity into deeper meaning through analysis and interpretation. (Howes, 1973, p. viii)

Unfortunately, many teachers, still unwilling or unable to follow the vigorous requirements of study, analysis, and prescription that the open school (or progressive school) demands, once again turned their classroom into approximations of those "gardens of enchantment for little people."

By the mid-1970s, parents discovered that their children were not learning the higher level cognitive skills of analysis and interpretation. Further, students could not even read. Silberman, who was perhaps more singularly responsible for beginning the open-school revolution, was quoted as saying:

> They literally broke down walls out of a mistaken idea that "open" means "open space." The noise level got so high that nobody knew what he was doing. They used programmed instruction which is not individual in the real sense. And they did it all without teacher training. It was chaos, and kids didn't learn a goddam thing. ("Back to Basics," 1974, p. 95)

The open classroom can be as effective as the British infants school, and as good as the progressive classrooms of John Dewey's era. The great-grandchildren of the first youngsters to study in Mr. and Mrs. Dewey's laboratory school at the University of Chicago still may run afoul of lazy or incompetent teaching disguised as the latest thing. Nothing in the concept of the open classroom prevents rigorous attention to mastering basics, such as the three Rs. Most parents and teachers would agree those skills will aid someone in the twenty-first as well as in this century. There is legitimate question about what other areas would be commonly agreed upon as basic. Is English grammar in that category? The dates of the Seven Years War? The multiplication table?

Programed and Computer-Assisted Instruction

Programed instruction cited by Silberman as not being "individual in the true sense" is exemplified in *individually prescribed instruction*. In sequential minilessons, material to be learned is broken into small factual segments, arranged sequentially, and interspersed with reinforcements in the form of feedback about correctness of response. This format is easily handled by a computer system. It may, however, also be found in printed form similar to a textbook of questions and answers. Whether in print or by computer terminal, the only way the technique permits individuality is in allowing the pupil to proceed at his or her individual rate through the same material as presented to everyone else. At present all computer-assisted lessons require *linear programs*, computer instructions that allow the student but one route or line to follow. In the future, computers may be able to be operated by *branch programs*, which would offer the student a choice of methods to master the same material. Bright children, for example, find the constant reinforcement of most programed materials interfers with their cognitive flow. They don't need constant feedback as reward and reinforcement. They could branch off into another program covering the same material but omitting the step-by-step feedback and reinforcement that characterizes most programed learning.

Other Instructional Media

Instruction by radio, television, movies, and video or audio tape cassettes all appear to help students learn at least as well as from a traditional teacher. As fairly recent innovations, there are few conclusive studies that indicate their superiority over the usual instruction by books and lecturers. Both individually prescribed instruction and computer-assisted instruction appear to save both student and teacher time. With rising costs, such savings are worthwhile, since they would release funds and efforts for some other allocation. (Dean Jamison et al., 1974)

Perhaps these shiny new educational toys are still being used in traditional ways; perhaps once again the same treatment has been applied, regardless of the individual student's aptitude or need. Combined with the refinements of an ATI approach, however, these new media may yet lead to the great forward leap in education that was predicted as each was introduced to the educational public.

Simulations and Games

Since learning can be defined as a change in behavior due to influences from the environment, teachers have frequently tried to induce learning by making changes in the physical as well as social environment. Gross examples of this are placing students into on-the-job vocational programs. The Philadelphia Parkway Program radically changed the learning environment by moving students right into the larger society.

Within classrooms, teachers have changed the social environment by using the technique of role playing. Students take parts in a relatively unstructured playlet as a method of better understanding human relationships. Sometimes, reversing the roles they have just played is even more effective in undoing students' perspectives for this gives them a firsthand experience of the attitudes and values of others.

Human relationships, values, and decisions, however, are also affected by factors of government and economics. A new educational method uses games and other *simulations* to introduce these facts into the role-playing situation. The popular game of Monopoly was an early (mid-1930s) and excellent example of how economic reality can be introduced into individual decision making. Some educational simulations can be exceedingly complex, as in the war games used to train future military officers. Computers can be utilized to print out descriptions of what the results of patterns of proposed decisions will be.

Simulations are especially useful in helping students to clarify or try out value systems in the process of making decisions. As discussed in Chapter 5, one of the most important needs of American youth as they confront the future is to be able to clarify, identify, and be influenced by a value system that they personally prize. Parents can and probably must assist the schools in this socialization task, but there is no question about its necessity. Human values are like wedges and ropes cast before us by which we can scale the mountain of tomorrow. Learning how to make proper value decisions may be the most basic task of all in transforming the schools for tomorrow.

MAIN IDEAS

1. While society and the overall school system regulate much of what can go on in a classroom, a classroom (teacher and pupils) is a complete social group and capable of initiating change.
2. In a traditional classroom decision making about tasks to be accomplished is in the hands of the teacher alone. Membership decisions are shared with pupils, and a teacher's skill in this area affects his or her success in getting tasks accomplished.
3. Role allocation is traditionally determined by the authority of the teacher with some influence from the social status of pupils. Inter- and intraclass grouping reflect role allocation.
4. Typically, the integrating function of the classroom is controlled by the discipline a teacher is able to maintain. There are several techniques for maintaining discipline, some more conducive than others to student maturation.

5. Since classroom communication reflects the nature of social interaction, several methods have been developed to study both verbal and nonverbal communications.
6. An often neglected aspect of the teacher's task of enculturating is a careful review of the many social factors that affect each individual's potential to adopt as his or her own the learning goals of the schoolroom.
7. The classroom system can be reformed through:
    a. A new multi-aptitude view of a child's school ability, as opposed to the old concept of a single age-linked ability
    b. New curricula combining skills and concepts from several disciplines
    c. A new view of the aims of education
    d. New role behavior on the part of teachers and students
8. Possible alternate forms of learning environment include:
    a. The open classroom
    b. Alternative instructional media
    c. Varying the learning environment by way of simulation techniques

GLOSSARY

aptitude-treatment interaction The psychological theory that human achievement can be maximized by highly individualized instruction (treatment) tailored to a wider variety of aptitudes than previously considered.

communication Processes between two (or more) systems providing information and feedback.

heterogeneous grouping Gathering students who have no planned characteristics in common into a class.

homogeneous grouping Gathering students who share a common characteristic, such as age or reading ability into a class.

role playing A technique in which persons play out various situations by adopting the variety of roles each situation demands.

simulation A technique that utilizes the facts of economics, government process, and the like, in classroom role playing in order to provide a more realistic learning environment.

sociogram A measure of group attractiveness revealed in responses to specific questions about group membership ties. These responses may be diagramed to show a picture of relationships among members.

SUGGESTED ACTIVITIES

1. Visit an open classroom or alternate school and analyze its structure and operations by using one of the models suggested in Chapter 1.

2. Use Flanders' and Bales' interaction analyses (see below) to compare and contrast student and teacher behavior in traditional and alternate classrooms.

3. Chart several of your college classes using the interaction analyses of Flanders or Bales summarized below. To what do you attribute differences—subject matter, the idiographic dimension of teacher role behavior, class size, or something else?

4. After studying a programed text, or a how-to-program instruction guide, attempt to write a programed lesson. Try the lesson out on several friends and observe individual differences in their responses.

5. Role play a classroom control situation utilizing traditional (usually punitive) and then Skinnerian concepts.

Flanders' Categories for Interaction Analysis

Teacher Talk

Indirect Influence
   *1. Accepts Feeling: accepts and clarifies the feeling tone of the students in a non-threatening manner. Feelings may be positive or negative. Predicting or recalling feelings are included.

*2. Praises or Encourages: praises or encourages student action or behavior. Jokes that release tension, not at the expense of another individual, nodding head or saying "um hum?" or "go on" are included.

*3. Accepts or Uses Ideas of Student: clarifying, building, or developing ideas suggested by a student. As teacher brings more of his own ideas into play, shift to category five.

Direct Influence

*4. Asks Questions: asking a question about content or procedure with intent that a student answer. Direct influence.

*5. Lecturing: giving facts or opinions about content or procedure; expressing his own ideas, asking rhetorical questions.

*6. Giving Directions: directions, commands, or orders with which a student is expected to comply.

*7. Criticizing or Justifying Authority: statements intended to change student behavior from non-acceptable to acceptable pattern; bawling someone out; stating why the teacher is doing what he is doing; extreme self-reference.

Student Talk

*8. Student Talk-Response: talk by students in response to teacher. Teacher initiates the contact or solicits student statement.

*9. Student Talk-Initiation: talk by students which they initiate. If "calling on" student is only to indicate who may talk next, observer must decide whether student wanted to talk. If he did, use this category.

*10. Silence or Confusion: pauses, short periods of silence, and periods of confusion in which communication cannot be understood by the observer.

---

*There is no scale implied by these numbers. Each number is classificatory; it designates a particular kind of communication event. To write these numbers down during observation is to enumerate, not to judge a position on a scale.
Source: Ned A. Flanders, *Teacher Influence, Pupil Attitudes and Achievements.* U.S. Department of Health, Education and Welfare, Office of Education, Cooperative Research Monograph No. 12, 1960.

Bales' Interaction Process Categories

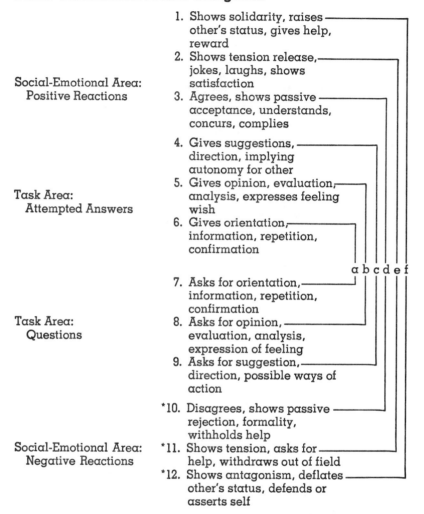

Social-Emotional Area: Positive Reactions	1. Shows solidarity, raises other's status, gives help, reward 2. Shows tension release, jokes, laughs, shows satisfaction 3. Agrees, shows passive acceptance, understands, concurs, complies
Task Area: Attempted Answers	4. Gives suggestions, direction, implying autonomy for other 5. Gives opinion, evaluation, analysis, expresses feeling wish 6. Gives orientation, information, repetition, confirmation
Task Area: Questions	7. Asks for orientation, information, repetition, confirmation 8. Asks for opinion, evaluation, analysis, expression of feeling 9. Asks for suggestion, direction, possible ways of action
Social-Emotional Area: Negative Reactions	*10. Disagrees, shows passive rejection, formality, withholds help *11. Shows tension, asks for help, withdraws out of field *12. Shows antagonism, deflates other's status, defends or asserts self

a b c d e f

Key: *a* – problems of orientation; *b* – problems of evaluation; *c* – problems of control; *d* – problems of decision; *e* – problems of tension-management; and *f* – problems of integration.

*In numbers 10, 11, and 12, Bales suggests that nonverbal behavior may also reflect group participation.

SOURCE: Robert Bales and Fred Strodbeck, "Phases in Group Problem Solving," *Journal of Abnormal and Social Psychology*, XLVI (1951), 486. Copyright 1951 by the American Psychological Association. Reprinted by permission.

BIBLIOGRAPHY

Atkinson, J. W. *An Introduction to Motivation.* Princeton, N.J.: Van Nostrand, 1964.

"Back to Basics." *Newsweek,* 21 October 1974, p. 95.

Bales, Robert, and Fred Strodbeck. "Phases in Group Problem Solving." *Journal of Abnormal and Social Psychology,* XLVI (1951), 485–95.

Barry, Herbert A., III, et al. "Relation of Child-Training to Subsistence Economy." *American Anthropologist,* LXI (1959), 51–63.

Boocock, Sarane S. *An Introduction to the Sociology of Learning.* Boston: Houghton Mifflin, 1972.

Cohen, Elizabeth G. "Sociology and the Classroom: Setting the Conditions for Teacher-Student Interaction." *Review of Educational Research,* XLII, 4 (Fall 1972), 441–52.

Flanders, Ned A. *Teacher Influence, Pupil Attitudes and Achievement.* U.S. Department of Health, Education and Welfare, Office of Education, Cooperative Research Monograph No. 12, 1960.

Galloway, Charles M. "Non-Verbal Teacher Behaviors: A Critique." *American Educational Research Journal,* II, 3 (Summer 1974), 305–6.

Glaser, Robert. "Individuals and Learning: The New Aptitudes." *Educational Researcher,* June 1972, pp. 5–13.

Greeley, Andrew M., and Peter H. Rossi. *The Education of Catholic Americans.* Chicago: Aldine, 1966.

Howes, Virgil. *Informal Teaching in the Open Classroom.* New York: Macmillan, 1973.

Jamison, Dean, et al. "The Effectiveness of Alternative Instructional Media: A Survey." *Review of Educational Research,* XLIV, 1 (Winter 1974), 1–67.

Kohlberg, Laurence. "Stages of Moral Development as a Basis for Moral Education." In *Moral Education.* Ed. C. M. Beck et al. Toronto: University of Toronto Press, 1971.

Lawler, Patricia R. Book review in *Educational Studies,* V, 1 and 2 (Spring/Summer 1974), 64.

Lintner, Alfred C., and Joseph DuCette. "The Effects of Locus of Control, Academic Failures and Task Dimensions on a Student's Responsiveness to Praise." *American Educational Research Journal,* II, 3 (Summer 1974), 231–39.

Rist, R. "The Self-Fulfilling Prophecy of the Ghetto School." *Harvard Educational Review,* XL, 7 (Summer 1970), 411–51.

Rogers, Carl R. "Forget You Were Ever a Teacher." *The Catechist,* September 1970, pp. 12, 34–35.

Rohwer, W. D., Jr. "Learning, Race and School Success." *Review of Educational Research*, XLI, (1971), 191–210.

Sexton, Patricia Cayo. *The American School, A Sociological Analysis.* Englewood Cliffs, N.J.: Prentice-Hall, 1967.

Silberman, Charles E. *Crisis in the Classroom: The Remaking of American Education.* New York: Vintage Books, 1970.

Skinner, B. F. *Walden Two.* New York: Macmillan, 1962.

Smith, L., and W. Geoffrey. *The Complexities of an Urban Classroom: An Analysis Toward a General Theory of Teaching.* New York: Holt, Rinehart and Winston, 1968.

Toffler, Alvin. *Future Shock.* New York: Bantam Books, 1970.

Walker, Decker F., and Jon Schaffarzick. "Comparing Curricula." *Review of Educational Research, XLIV, 1 (Winter 1974), 83*–111.

Woolfolk, Robert L., and Anita E. Woolfolk. "Effects of Teacher Verbal and Nonverbal Behaviors on Student Perceptions and Attitudes." *American Educational Research Journal*, II, 3 (Summer 1974), 297ff.

Transformation for Tomorrow

CAN WE DETERMINE THE FUTURE?

Marshall McLuhan describes human beings as speeding into the future while looking in a rearview mirror. His description is particularly apt when applied to the public-school system. The past is studied extensively, the present is studied a little, but the future almost not at all—yet this is the dimension in which we all shall live.

What can you study about the future? Is it not so unknown or unknowable that there is no way of preparing for it? Some feel that the way the world looks now, perhaps it would be better *not* to study what's coming our way. Alvin Toffler believes there is a real conspiracy of silence in the schools—a conspiracy not to discuss the future.

Believing that present choices will determine that future at least in part, many scientists are beginning to develop ways of studying the future. And some educators are convinced that students can be better taught how to survive in the coming days, no matter what they may hold. So this final chapter of *Transforming Schools* attempts to break the conspiracy of silence. It will examine what teachers, schools, and pupils may do to prepare for tomorrow.

Some Past Thoughts about the Future

In 1857 Charles Darwin published a book in which he described a revolutionary theory about the nature of life on earth. *The Origin of Species* set forth the theory of evolution. This belief holds that each species (and each individual within the species) is fit for its environment in varying degrees. Those who are most fit survive to perpetuate their kind, while the least fit die off. Through the millions of years of life on earth, species after species that has failed to adapt has died, to be followed by other life forms that are better able to live in the changing environments of earth. Life on earth is not static, but a dynamic procession moving toward more and more superior forms.

This scientific idea formed the basis of the philosophy developed by Herbert Spencer. Spencer preached that progress was inevitable and the future rosy for those who would adapt. While Spencer was influencing political thinkers, economic thinkers watched the spread of industrial capitalism over the known world. Some influential economists developed theories based on the concept of unlimited growth in production and consumption of material goods.

Suddenly (or so it seemed), in the mid-twentieth century, this optimistic view of the future was confronted with some hard facts. In the atomic bomb, nations discovered a weapon that could kill not only their enemies, but in the fallout from radioactive clouds, their allies and themselves. Indeed, all species of life on earth could be wiped out. Thus the gradual upward movement of evolution would be brought to an abrupt halt. Within a generation of this atomic discovery, humans came to realize that the fuels and minerals upon which advanced civilization was based were being used up at a rate that would soon eliminate earth's supplies. And the speed with which these resources were being utilized was polluting the air and water upon which all animals and plants depended for life.

With such realizations the optimism about progress of the century from 1850 to 1950 began to dissolve in smog. Characteristically, the pendulum of human thinking swung in the opposite direction. "Gloom and doom" were fashionable watchwords about the future of spaceship earth. Even successes were seen as problems. Prolonging life has led to overpopulation, affluence to increased pollution, advances in communication and transportation to an incapacity to handle all the ideas disseminated. (Willie Harriman, 1974)

When one looks over the entire course of human history, a more balanced view than unadulterated optimism or pessimism seems the most realistic view of the future. With the atomic bomb comes atomic energy, which in its fusionable form is both cheap and clean, freeing us from dependence on the fossil fuels we have consumed so greedily. Utilization of energy from the sun is even cheaper, and less polluting. Solar energy has the further benefit of being available directly to users, without the intervention of huge corporations to produce and distribute it.

Computerization and miniaturization, which can speed intercontinental missiles to their targets, may also result someday in production of material goods in small factories or workshops that are not so spirit-destroying as massive assembly lines. Community-produced radios and TVs can be put in billions of hands, for example.

The so-called "green revolution" has doubled and tripled rice and wheat yields in countries where famine has been endemic since man's recorded history. Scientists believe famine may be able to be eliminated within this century. The problem appears to be one of distribution rather than production.

The late industrial period in which we are living calls for massive international corporations and labor unions, with powerful national governments to complement them. Yet, solar energy, computerization and miniaturization, and the "green revolution" may soon permit goods to be produced and distributed in much smaller units. (Murray Bookshin, 1971) It is possible that human communities, now swollen to accommodate the proliferation of industrialism, can shrink again toward the intimacy of small face-to-face groups with their greater warmth and socio-emotional support of members.

Futurists—those who study where we may be heading—have already begun to describe the near future in quite different terms. One of them, Daniel Bell, coined the term that we have used throughout, the "postindustrial society" to describe the not-so-distant world where distribution and individualism assume the importance that production and standardization have had in the late industrial period. The conditions that have fostered bureaucracy are withering away.

The world of the distant future may be a *utopia*, or ideal place, as well as a *distopia*, or disaster-ridden region. The experts simply are not clear on the direction life will take. Robert Heilbroner wrote an optimistic volume in 1970, *The Future as History*, and in 1974 a pessimistic one, *An Inquiry into the Human Prospect*. The Club of Rome, a group of futurists from many countries, produced *The Year 2000* in 1970 and pessimistically buried starving mankind in pollution. A scant four years later, they acknowledged a variety of possibilities and could even see benefit in the oil-restricting policies of the Arab nations.

What the experts do agree on is that the future is not determined without input from human beings. Our choices will in part shape the future. What sort of a world to we want? What values should be conveyed to students to help them choose the future they want?

WHAT DO WE KNOW ABOUT THE FUTURE?

Many volumes have been written about the future in addition to those mentioned above. Some are based on facts and mathematical projections; others range toward prophetic insight. Some futurists see science fiction as a major source of knowledge about the world to come. The book about the future that has attained the greatest popular distribution in the United States is Alvin Toffler's *Future Shock* (1970).

Future shock is the physiological and psychological reaction humans have when they are bombarded with more new data than they can make meaningful. Think of a person as a self-programing computer, that is, as a machine capable of interpreting all the data that flows into it. According to Toffler, all human beings are now receiving masses of information, or input, from the environment. Not all these data can be accommodated on their present cognitive programs, and humans have precious little time to develop new programs while more and more data is flooding in. In situations like this, humans (like computers) break down. A prerequisite for survival is to learn to live with constant, pervasive change.

Toffler identified three characteristics of the foreseeable future that account for the present overload—novelty, transience, and diversity. While these characteristics already pervade all of human society today, the schools can provide good examples of each.

Novelty is reflected in the many new courses that are now included in the school curriculum. The specific content may cover material literally unknown to the parents of the children enrolled: computer programing, study of the DNA molecule, atomic energy, solid-state circuitry. If these seem on the fringe, consider the novel aspects of a traditional course like home economics. Shall we cook Italian, Chinese, "soul," or Greek? This is a decision our parents never had to make, no matter how pleasant, and our own ethnic background can hardly prepare us for the choice. Decisions such as this may be trivial, but when multiplied they can induce much anxiety.

Transience, or lack of permanence, may also produce anxiety and, indeed, is a real factor in today's schools, especially among lower-class children. The schools to date have done little to cope with this fringe of tomorrow. Toffler notes some of its effects:

> A recent study of high school students by Harry R. Moore of the University of Denver indicated that the test scores of children who had moved across state or county lines from one to ten times were not substantially different from those of children who had not. But there was a definite tendency for the more nomadic children to avoid participation in the voluntary side of school life—clubs, sports, student government and other extracurricular activities. It is as though they wished, where possible, to avoid new human ties that might have to be broken again before long—as if they wished, in short, to slow down the flow-through of people in their lives. (Toffler, 1970, p. 122)

A final characteristic, diversity, is everywhere in the minicourses and modular schedules of today's schools. We also spread before youth an array of 20,000 kinds of jobs from which they may choose a career—or at least their first career, for the odds are that they will change the type of work they do several times in one lifetime.

What will future citizens need to know to live in the society of tomorrow? In a world characterized by novelty, transience, and diversity, they surely do not need to know facts that deal with a fast dying or already dead past. The knowledge for the future must be skill- not fact-oriented.

The Skills We Will Need

Many modern educators now believe that the way to equip our children to live in the future is to change our view of education from a teaching process to a learning process. Here is how one original thinker puts it:

> [Learning] is an active process which necessitates full and aware participation. At times, learning included some training. Training is a teacher-centered activity; it deals with information known; known that is to the teacher. Learning is a learner-centered activity in which the learner deals with the unknown. It is more comfortable to deal with the known, which is, presumably why this is the primary method used to "educate" people. But it does not adequately prepare people to deal with the future—which is the unknown. (Donald Barnes, 1972, p. 13)

No matter what the curriculum, no matter who the student, certain skills must be learned to survive in the future. Each of them has already been introduced in preceding chapters as a response to avoid educational entropy in the present. Carried forward in time, they can also prepare youth for tomorrow.

Learning How to Learn. Especially because of the exploding world of vocational opportunity, where changes may be expected to continue, new workers must learn that education does not cease upon graduation. It is indeed a commencement, or beginning, and much new knowledge lies ahead. They will have to learn new skills for new jobs throughout adult life. Further, some old ideas will have to be unlearned, such as who is responsible for household chores. And some skills will have to be relearned—perhaps how to "play" after retirement in early middle age with a score of active years ahead.

Barnes, who was quoted above, believes one of the most essential learnings that must take place is for individuals to see themselves as active learners rather than passive recipients of teaching. He describes a three-point program as the "DOR" to this new role—disorientation (that is, unlearning the old role), orientation, and reorientation. This program would serve as a vestibule for students moving from traditional learning to new learning methods.

Learning How to Relate. Like the children in the quotation from Toffler above who were afraid to establish relationships with their new schoolmates, tomorrow's citizens must learn to establish satisfying relationships with many people whom they will meet in their changing roles. The constant face-to-face contacts of the village are gone (at least for a while), and many of our companions now are with us only for a little while, or a little piece of our lives. We don't have time for a slow development of rapport—both parties shall be on to new relationships too soon. As we move from place to place, job to job, role to role, we must relate quickly, skillfully, and satisfyingly.

Another aspect of relating deals with an individual's self-concept or sense of personal identity. In teaching children to relate more skillfully, schools must also help children to relate to a view of themselves as adults. Benjamin Singer calls this a "future-focused role image." (Singer, 1974). With this model of what they wish to be before them, the young are better able to make the proper choices to bring that model into reality.

Future schools may emphasize this membership or socio-emotional dimension much more than the traditional school. Barnes' DOR program, for instance, emphasizes noncognitive activities for relearning one's student role. He calls for outdoor challenges, such as the "Outward Bound" program, which provides near-survival challenges in wilderness settings. Another program, an audio-visual project by three educational honorary societies, has sought to improve elementary children's self-concept (and thus their achievement) through sequential physical exercises. ("Cooperative Activity Produces 'Yes I Can,'" 1974) Thinking may begin with feeling.

Learning How to Choose. One may learn techniques for marshaling facts, for increasing one's objectivity, for projecting possible outcomes of decisions. Choosing in and for itself is an important skill, most especially for those who live in a democracy and have a direct or indirect role in decision making. But there is another dimension beyond these factual considerations that must also be learned.

Learning How to Value. Decision also involves a selection among alternatives based on a normative or valuing dimension. Clarity as to *why* we make certain decisions, and whether we prize the outcome, permits better direction of future decisions.

It is through instruction in the skills of choosing and valuing that the established school can provide a counterbalance for the values being taught by the mass media. As stressed in Chapter 4, the mass media have no adequate check or balance upon their presentations. But their purveying of partial or selected facts and hedonistic values can be put in proper perspective by students who are skilled in the valuing process.

HOW CAN SCHOOLS CHANGE TO MEET THE NEEDS OF THE FUTURE?

Throughout this book we have noted how little public schools have changed in the century and a half since their establishment. They are still geared to meet the needs of an industrialized society, stressing the values of conformity and submissiveness, when our society is shifting radically to a postindustrial one in which individuality and independent action are more necessary. If the futurists we have just described are correct, many changes are rapidly taking place. So it is imperative to transform the educational establishment now. Can it be done?

Students of the future have identified three major ways that schools may be transformed to better meet the requirements of future citizens. Some changes are relatively easy and may be begun at once; others are extremely difficult and will take a long period of time if they are ever to be accomplished.

Changing the Process

A primary change already suggested is a renewed emphasis upon the learning process, especially an emphasis upon those four skills just outlined above. If a classroom teacher cannot justify a procedure on the basis of learning how to learn, relate, choose, or value, the procedure is probably robbing valuable time and effort from more productive activities.

Changing the Curriculum

Curriculum changes were discussed by a variety of contributors in *Learning for Tomorrow*, a book that Toffler compiled in 1974. Many suggested placing teaching about the future at the heart of contemporary studies. Such a change in subject matter may have a substantial impact on transforming schools into places of learning rather than teaching. As Decker Walker and Jon Schaffarzick point out, educators should:

> stop thinking of the curriculum as a fixed race course and begin to think of it as a tool, apparently a powerful one, for stimulating and directing the active learning capacities which are ultimately responsible for the achievement we want from schools. (Walker and Schaffarzick, 1974, p. 109)

Curriculum in this light is seen as a way of maximizing the motivation of students to want to learn the essential skills of learning, relating, choosing, and valuing. Dates in past history quite naturally motivate fewer pupils than hypothesizing about future events they may someday experience firsthand. This is not by any means to suggest that the future be the *only* subject matter. Rather, content should be selected that directly fosters the learning of the central skills. The content may even be about the past. Social studies simulations are an example of activities that may have intrinsic value in fostering choosing and valuing skills, though the content may be past-directed.

Another method of curriculum reform that maximizes student interest and self-motivation involves reworking the subject matter deemed essential into *learning activities packets* (sometimes called "unipaks" or some other title). Essentially, these units are made up of a pretest, behavioral objectives, suggested activities, and a posttest. The material is usually prepared by teachers, but can be created by students. Every student selects a small unit that is of interest, sets himself or herself to the pretesting, and then selects activities suited to his or her learning style. Successful completion of the unit means passing the posttest. After that the student is ready to go on to other units, again freely selected. Certification indicates completion of units, not how long it takes the student to do the task or how well or ill he or she does relative to other students. One school in a center-city area found that while this form of curriculum organization did not necessarily improve achievement in the curriculum area, reading achievement shot up— possibly because it was a prerequisite for completing each unit. ("Project Expansion," 1974)

Changing the System

Educational sociologists from Sexton to Boocock have been quoted previously in this book as saying there can be no real change in the life of the schools unless the bureaucratic structure of the school can be displaced.

In this last decade of reform, however, there has been little evidence that structural change is in fact occurring. Joseph Giacquinta recently found that there were extraordinarily few changes in the structure of the 18,000 school systems of the United States. (Giacquinta, 1973) Another survey also uncovered few changes in structure, and almost no successful changes in transposing innovation from one district to another. (*Assessing Educational Innovations*, 1974)

There are two apparent reasons for the extreme difficulty encountered in changing a school system. First, as we noted when we discussed efforts to make teachers accountable, it is extremely difficult to measure the exact worth of a teacher's work in quantitative terms. Similarly, when plans are made for school change, it is difficult to come up with figures that will measure either inputs or outcomes.

There are some mathematical models for educational planning (see, for example, James Johnstone, 1974), but they measure clearly quantifiable variables such as school enrollments and never touch on more nebulous variables such as classroom atmosphere.

B. F. Skinner and his followers have taken us a long way down the road toward behavioral objectives, but many teacher goals remain outside these measurable criteria. Further, we do not now know how to isolate or measure many factors that go into the mix of student and teacher personalities or learning/ teaching styles.

Previous prescriptions for change have been based on a model of school structure that is static and mechanistic. Here and there, students of educational reform are now envisioning the school as a constantly fluctuating, dynamic biosystem that demands other methods of analysis. As Jacob Getzels outlined as early as 1963, a social system cannot be studied solely in terms of its parts, nor can it be viewed as a totality. In a healthy biosystem, each constantly transforms the other.

Within this perspective, one possible solution to the dilemma of educational change is to move from reforms that focus on being comprehensive and prescriptive to plans that deal with smaller pieces of the educational scene and attempt to make modifications piecemeal over time. (Frank Schmidtlein, 1974) This may be a more realistic way of coping with a biosystem that is constantly assimilating and accommodating as changes are made within it and about it.

Two examples of this approach suggest its usefulness in educational planning. A 1975 article on the management of educational research focuses on strategies that could reach "beyond bureaucracy." (Ronald Corwin, 1975) In place of the rigid hierarchy of current educational research and development agencies, a network of common-interest peers is envisioned (The concept of network is a key component of the ideas of Ivan Illich, as we shall discuss in greater detail below.)

Transforming change across the boundaries of a school system is suggested by John Pincus of the Rand Corporation, a California "think tank" where alternative solutions to contemporary problems are probed. After a searching analysis of incentives for change in public schools, Pincus pessimistically concludes that innovations that in any way appear to threaten the basic structure of the school bureaucracy will be treated like fads or ignored. (Pincus, 1974)

His concrete recommendation, however, is the establishment of a network-like coalition with county and state officials, since they represent one form (a legitimate form) of outside pressure that can be brought to bear on school officials. Estes Nolan, the innovative superintendent of the Dallas public schools, brought his board and the city council together in a *common* problem-solving workshop centering on school problems.

EDUCATION WITHOUT SCHOOLS

An eminent historian of education, Lawrence Cremin, has been reminding school people for years that schools are far from the only educative force in society. As a matter of fact, the American public school is a quite recent invention, scarcely 150 years old. But families and churches and books and public fairs have been educating humans for centuries. (Fred Hechinger, 1974) These institutions socialized the young before the establishment of the American common school in the mid-nineteenth century; they continue to educate youth today and will undoubtedly continue to do so tomorrow.

More modern means are also available. The information sources of the mass media can be combined with a computer terminal so that students can respond and two-way communication can be established. This improves learning because immediate feedback permits auto-regulation. We may expect much of the required factual knowledge of our culture (such as the three Rs) to be taught technologically. While such technological teaching may not be better than the classroom teacher (Dean Jamison, 1974), it is much cheaper. School investment in this machinery saves labor costs in the form of teacher salaries. When cost effectiveness is important, educational administrators will surely be tempted to opt for what economists call "capital intensive" investment, that is, a bigger investment in machinery than in laborers.

Maximization and utilization of the mass media as a teaching tool has occurred in Great Britain where the *open university* permits adults to combine TV viewing, home experimentation, and attendance at neighborhood centers into a significant university experience. In this program, the electronic media are combined with small peer group meetings and one-to-one contact between learner and expert. The open university is a good example of a second out-of-school educative force gaining increasing significance—*adult socialization*. Traditionally families and schools are responsible for educating youth. As long as the society of adults is the same as the society the youth are expected to inherit, such socialization is practical. What we see today, however, is the growing significance of socialization by peer groups—not the peer groups of puberty and adolescence, but adult peers. As we noted in Chapter 5, this is what anthropologist Margaret Mead calls cofigurative socialization.

This theme of adult socialization by peer adults occurred and recurred in a recent conference on "Social Change and Social Character." (University of Delaware, 3, 4 October 1974) Anthropologists, psychologists, and sociologists cited various examples of how the values of the cultural revolution, the so-called youth rebellion, of the mid-1960s had spread to the rest of the population—from peer to peer, from adult to adult. Most of this dissemination of the change in values was informal; that is, it was unplanned and transmitted in face-to-face conversation. The growth of continuing education in its many forms is an example of planned and formal adult socialization. It results from the ever-increasing need for various forms of resocializing adult members in American society.

Deschooling Society

It seems quite clear that adult socialization can continue without a formal educational structure, but can the same be said for socialization of the young? That is, could society survive without schools?

Pressures for reformation of the educational system accelerated as a result of the publication in 1971 of *Deschooling Society* by Ivan Illich. Charged with preparing missionaries to work in the underdeveloped nations of South America, Illich acquired a new view of established schools as *causing* rather than resulting from the rigidity and impersonality of modern technological society.

It is Illich's belief that an adequate educational system could be composed of four facets that are built upon the presently active out-of-school forces. (1) By the time schools finally close their doors, society could have established computer-keyed networks of persons, experts in the required field, who would be available as resources to those who specifically request their help. (2) There would also be networks and repositories of things—something like our present-day libraries, but vastly expanded to comprise much nonprint material and tools of every variety. Individuals might borrow and use these tools as they saw fit. (3) Since Illich believes in the importance of learning by sharing perspectives with other searchers, there would be a network of peers whom people could readily identify and join with to discuss what they had learned via resource persons or electronic tools. Contact with all these resources would be solely on the initiative of the learners, and at that point when they themselves felt a real need to learn.

This sort of self-motivation suggests a certain maturity of personality. Indeed, Illich's perspective is that of adult education. Probably because Illich's background is in training adult educators for developing countries where the previous education of adults is sometimes nonexistent, the young would be involved only when they are sufficiently adult to see their own needs and have the desire to fulfill them. (4) Illich *does* see a need for a primary school where little children would be brought together in a more conventional school setting in order to receive instruction in the most basic skills of literacy.

Bridges to Deschooling

Converts to Illich's vision have the problem of bridging the gap between education as it is today and as it would be in his society of the future. But the nucleus for some of his ideas already exists. Networks of resource persons and peers with common interests have been established and can be located not only in radical educational publications such as *Out-of-the-Net*, but also through the classified columns of such venerable and establishment magazines as *Harper's*. There are also now networks of educational researchers who try to overcome the entropic tendencies of bureaucratic organization. For example, Dallas Superintendent Nolan, mentioned above, also established a network of fellow superintendents to open up the educational system. He warned, however, against such groups becoming exclusive. "One conclusion those superintendents came to was that the urban school superintendent, to survive, had to participate in decisions outside the school system." (Nolan,

1974, p. 24) No real networks of things exist, though perhaps the utilization of the resources of Philadelphia's Parkway (see Chapter 6) was a step in this direction.

A change in the curriculum of two Minnesota high schools precipitated a change in the methods of learning that illustrates how Illich's ideas could be approached from the springboard of the traditional school. A course entitled "Futuristics, Theory and Application" was set up for selected juniors and seniors in place of the standard English and social studies requirements. (Penny Damlo, 1974) The course was scheduled after lunch each day, which freed the students to leave school after half a day and go out into the community to work with the particular resource person knowledgeable in the field the student wanted to study. The schools are near to the Twin Cities of Minneapolis and St. Paul, so the students could call upon all the personnel of the city and state governments, the University of Minnesota and the several other institutions of higher learning there, as well as a group of technologically advanced industries. In order to receive credit for their individual projects, however, each student had to polish his or her presentation before classmates and then share knowledge gained with some other group—another class in school, a PTA, a Girl Scout troop—thus participating in cofigurative transmission of knowledge.

It is interesting to note that, as might be expected, support for this program came originally from outside the school system. The Sperry-Rand/Univac Corporation prevailed upon the schools and community to support this program. Further, the barrier between the two school systems, and the barrier that frequently exists between high schools and colleges, was breached by utilization of the Science Museum of Minnesota. This institution had ties to several levels of the educational bureaucracy without being an actual part of any individual hierarchy. A museum, of course, is a prototype of Illich's "network of things."

It is difficult to imagine a program such as this one being organized in areas where there are markedly fewer resource persons available. Indeed, it is difficult to imagine all the juniors and seniors in these two high schools participating, much less all the upper grade students in the Twin Cities area. This program does suggest, however, how the public schools may be transformed piece by piece, that is, incrementally, rather than attempting to change a school, a system, or the educational establishment wholesale.

TRANSFORMING SCHOOLS

Possibly, as the schools' severest critics contend, there is no way to reform or transform the American public school so that it properly accomplishes the role it has been allocated—the socialization of youth for today and tomorrow. But, as the title of this book suggests, we do not think so. We have some suggested routes to follow, which spring from the assumptions of our transformational model. First, schools, as biological systems, are dynamic. They do change over time. The technique for transforming them is to select a future-focused model and to move incrementally toward it. As Barnes suggests, a sequence of stages may be required, such as the DOR period he recommends. Massive, quickly conceived, and quickly instituted changes apparently neither survive nor are able to be transplanted in the field of education. Too much change threatens the "human computer" and induces future shock. A teacher ought not to be disheartened by beginning within the single frame of a classroom. This may be the most manageable and effective unit for change.

For those of you who wish to be "inside change agents working from below" (read, teachers), Ronald Havelock's *The Change Agent's Guide to Innovation in Education* (1973) is a useful handbook. This book adopts a step-by-step and extraordinary specific approach to move education from "the way it is now" to "the way we would like it to be in the future." The perspective, however, is a modest and practical one, which assumes the traditional public-school system.

Another method for transforming the school structure is to open it up to the society it serves. Specifically, a teacher as a member of a professional organization can join forces working to make the schools more vital. Teachers can come to know the local labor organizer, the industrial lobbyist at the state house, the names and voting records of their representatives in Congress. These forces outside the system can force a change within it. Professional expertise will be welcomed if offered in cooperation and with acknowledgment of common concern. Overtures to local college personnel may bring their expertise to bear upon the "peer elite," that is, the bureaucratic decision makers in a school.

In the area of decision making, school bureaucracies themselves, like other modern organizations, are having to invent ways (such as networks) to get around the rules and regulations of their own operational systems. Toffler identified the network of committees set up to accomplish one particular task but whose impact reaches across the stratifications of bureaucracy as the "ad hocracy." Change-agent teachers will volunteer to work on such committees and work when they get there. And when they leave, they will work to get its recommendations adopted throughout the system. Decision making on such committees moves the system toward a new form of school organization that Barnes described:

> Administrative functions needed to keep the system functioning —not to control it or set policy—would be parceled out to various people. Management accountability would be achieved by a few full-time administrative people selected from and by the total community of learners who would serve only for a year or two. (Barnes, 1972, p. 19)

Massive educational bureaucracies could gradually be deflated as more modern methods of decision making are substituted.

Transformation also depends on refocusing school responsibility from one that emphasizes the task or cognitive dimension of learning to one that elevates the membership or socioemotional variables to equal status. Learning how to relate and how to value others and oneself are essential skills in and for themselves in the world of the future. A tolerable future will result from humanity's developing skills in these areas, not from the increasing use of technology. Further, it appears that true cognitive excellence can only be accomplished when supported by a realistic and positive self-concept. In other words, in order to accomplish the cognitive, task-dimension skills of learning how to learn and learning how to decide, schools must increase the attention they give to learning how to relate and how to value.

A major key to change appears to lie in a redefinition of the reciprocal roles of students and teachers. As pupils are assisted to see themselves as the heart of the learning process, teachers must keep in mind that the status and authority of their ascribed role are based upon knowledge of material that may be completely irrelevant tomorrow. To repeat the significant advice of Carl Rogers, "Forget you are a teacher."

Finally, transformation also demands that teachers shift their attention from groups of children to the individual pupil. In the person is the place, source, and reason for learning. Perhaps ultimately this is what is most meant when it is recommended that schools change their focus from teaching to learning.

If you wish to aid in the transformation for tomorrow, the best place to begin is with each of the uniquely individual youth whom society places in your care.

MAIN IDEAS

1. The future may be studied, though in the past such studies have been overly optimistic or pessimistic.
2. We know that the immediate future will be marked by novelty, transience, and diversity. These attributes may bring on "future shock."
3. Skills we will need for the future include learning how to learn, relate, choose, and value.
4. Schools can change to meet future needs by:
   a. renewed emphasis on learning processes
   b. curriculum changes to improve motivation
   c. changes in the educational system
5. Education can take place without schools.
6. Some suggested methods for transforming schools are:
   a. focusing upon small, incremental steps toward change
   b. breaking through barriers that separate the school and society
   c. getting around educational bureaucracy through effective "ad hocracy"
   d. stressing socio-emotional as well as task variables

   e. redefining the reciprocal roles of students and teachers

   f. focusing upon the individual learner

GLOSSARY

adult socialization Formal and informal methods of transmitting cultural change among adults.

distopia A disastrous future world.

future shock A physiological and psychological reaction to an overload of information input into the human system.

futurists Persons who study possible futures and ways to move toward them.

learning activities packets Learning units composed of pretests, behavioral objectives, suggested activities, and posttests that students select and complete on their own.

open university A new concept in education that allows adults to obtain college credit by participation in a program that combines TV viewing, home experimentation, and attendance at group meetings in local neighborhoods.

utopia An ideal future world.

SUGGESTED ACTIVITIES

1. Check *The Futurist*, the journal of the World's Future's Society, to see if there is a local chapter of the society nearby where you can participate in a meeting.

2. Printed materials about possible futures presently abound. Select some economic or social aspect and analyze its impact upon education.

3. Attempt to identify your personal view of utopia. What would education be like in that society?

4. Many school personnel will be willing to discuss innovative practices with you. Attempt to identify the reasons for change, the likelihood of their success in terms of sociological reality, the assumptions about future needs these innovations are planned to meet. What methods for evaluation are planned? Are the changes significant, and if so, were they instituted by the school's established structure?

5. Educational planners are learning new future-oriented techniques for analysis and projection. What are some of these techniques? You might wish to share your study with your classmates.

6. Almost every large industry has a research and development (R & D) arm. Interview a research staff member to see if the techniques he or she describes can be utilized in an educational setting.

7. Probably you have planned to be a teacher for at least several years. You chose this career because the models of role behavior you saw seemed to appeal to you. Now you are counseled to "forget you are a teacher"—to forget the teacher models of your own youth. Can you, or *do* you want to, become a "facilitator of learning" instead? (Is such a question "an activity"? Arriving at a personally valid answer may be the *most* significant activity of your semester's work.)

BIBLIOGRAPHY

Assessing Educational Innovations. Eugene: ERIC Clearinghouse on Educational Management, University of Oregon, 1974.

Barnes, Donald. *Learning Systems for the Future.* Bloomington, Ind.: Phi Delta Kappan Educational Foundation, 1972.

Bookshin, Murray. *Post Scarcity Anarchism.* Berkeley, Calif.: Ramparts Press, 1971.

Cohen, Elizabeth G. "Sociology and the Classroom: Setting the Conditions for Teacher-Student Interaction." *Review of Educational Research*, XLII, 4 (Fall 1972), 441–52.

"Cooperative Activity Produces 'Yes I Can.'" *Executive Secretary's Memo*, from Lowell C. Rose, Phi Delta Kappan, V, 3 (October 1974), 1.

Corwin, Ronald G. "Beyond Bureaucracy in Educational Research Management." *The Generator of Division G*, American Educational Research Association, V, 2 (Winter 1975), 3–12.

Damlo, Penny. "Futuristics Cures 'Doomsday Syndrome.' " *The Futurist*, VIII, 4 (August 1974), 183–84.

Giacquinta, Joseph B. "The Process of Organization Change in Schools." In *Review of Research in Education*. Ed. Fred N. Kerlinger. Itasca, Ill.: F. E. Peacock, 1973. I, 178–200.

Harriman, Willie W. "The Coming Transformation in Our View of Knowledge." *The Futurist*, VIII, 3 (June 1974), 126–28.

Havelock, Ronald G. *The Change Agent's Guide to Innovation in Education*. Englewood Cliffs, N.J.: Educational Technology Publications, 1973.

Hechinger, Fred M. "Lawrence Cremin: Looking Toward the Heights." *SR/World*, 19 October 1974, pp. 54–55.

Hill, Joseph E. *How Schools Can Apply Systems Analysis*. Bloomington, Ind.: Phi Delta Kappan Educational Foundation, 1972.

Illich, Ivan. *Deschooling Society*. New York: Harper & Row, 1971.

Jamison, Dean, et al. "The Effectiveness of Alternative Instructional Media: A Survey." *Review of Educational Research*, XLIV, 1 (Winter 1974), 1–67.

Johnstone, James N. "Mathematical Models Developed for Use in Educational Planning. A Review." *Review of Educational Research*, XLIV, 2 (Spring 1974), 177–201.

Nolan, Estes. "Marshalling Community Leadership to Support the Public Schools." Bloomington, Ind.: Phi Delta Kappan Educational Foundation, 1974.

Pincus, John. "Incentives for Innovation in the Public Schools." *Review of Educational Research*, XLIV, 1 (Winter 1974), 113–44.

"Project Expansion." Personal communication from H. E. Wilson, Director, Wilmington, Delaware, Public Schools, 1974.

Sarason, Seymour B. *The Culture of the School and the Problem of Change*, Boston: Allyn & Bacon, 1971.

Schmidtlein, Frank A. "Decision Process Paradigms in Education." *Educational Researcher*, May 1974, pp. 4–10.

Singer, Benjamin D. "The Future-Focused Role Image." In *Learning for Tomorrow, The Role of the Future in Education*. Ed. Alvin Toffler. New York: Vintage Books, 1974, pp. 19–32.

Toffler, Alvin. *Future Shock*. New York: Bantam Books, 1970.

——, ed. *Learning for Tomorrow, The Role of the Future in Education* New York: Vintage Books, 1974.

Walker, Decker, and Jon Schaffarzick. "Comparing Curricula." *Review of Educational Research*, XLIV, 1 (Winter 1974), 83–111.

Index